TWO
CENTS

For Carol —
I pray you'll enjoy
journeying through
Two Cents. Blessings!
Linda
Psalm 100

TWO CENTS

Generational wisdom without all the fuss

Compiled and Comments by

LINDA C. ROWGO

To those I love

Father God
*For Your unconditional love, patience, goodness,
and wee-hour tutorials*

Jesus
My very best Friend

Russ and Mara
Whose encouragement and love are priceless and such a blessing

My grandchildren and great-grands
The beat goes on

My for-real, safe friends
Who bless me with teeter-totter reciprocity

ACKNOWLEDGMENTS

Enormous thanks go to my gifted and technology-savvy son, Russ Rowgo, who took my basic words and formatted the whole shebang. Without his skills, *Two Cents* would have remained locked in my laptop for eternity.

Greatly blessed by my daughter, Mara Rowgo McClellan, who has bounced ideas off with me and helped me develop as a wordsmith. When we talk, time stands still. We laugh, cry, pray, and love extravagantly.

Thanks to MollyAnn Wymer Stinson for the very kind and affirming Foreword. She has been such an inspiration and support to me over the past few years and has even become my "bonus daughter."

Two Cents was compiled "with a lot of help from my friends"—both known and unknown. Without the words appearing online in the first place, I never would have been inspired to add my two cents and turn it into a book. Thanks for the major nudge!

My mom, Christine Zichterman Schrier, relocated to Heaven in 2005, but the essence of the impact she left on my life always remains with me. Her legacy will live on through the words, thoughts, deeply rooted faith, and perspectives offered throughout this book.

TABLE OF CONTENTS

FOCUSED OUTWARD

FOCUSED UPWARD

FINAL THOUGHTS

FOREWORD

Maybe you know Linda. Maybe you've sat and shared stories. You may have come to her in an hour of desperation, like I did, and found not only wisdom, but compassion, solace, help, and guidance. You may have found like I did, true friendship.

I don't think that Linda would mind me saying that her "days are numbered." My days are numbered and so are yours. I believe it is the knowledge of her mortality that urged her to write down all that she has learned, all she feels may need repeating, all the "two cents" that she's given over her lifetime.

I say it's been "freely given," but anyone with hard-earned wisdom knows that life wisdom often comes at the great cost of personal experiences. I am thankful that Linda is leaving a very summarized legacy of some of her most valuable "two cents."

If you could put a value on the experience and wisdom and understanding of each page, what did it actually cost her? Is there a celestial calculator? *Yes, there actually is.* Humility begs that she downplay the value of the words in these pages; wisdom begs that the reader stop, think, breathe, and calculate.

Linda's life—the lives of every person she has laughed with, cried with, prayed over, and labored with for real life healing and change—is the cusp of which is found in these pages. I am almost insulted at her chosen title... (not really, but a little). *Two Cents*... Linda, Linda, Linda... maybe two cent pieces made of diamonds... maybe.

I pray your numbered days remain in the favor of all of us that love you, need you, and thank God for you. We still need fresh "two-cent diamonds" to add season to our lives.

MollyAnn Wymer Stinson
Author of *Becoming Fearless*

INTRODUCTION

For years, I've had a niggling urge to write a book, but I dismissed the thought. What could I possibly write about that hadn't already been covered by countless others? My viewpoint or take on things may have a bit of a different twist on things, but so what? And then came Facebook. Oh my! The plethora of posts triggered so many revelations, thoughts, and emotions in me. They were full of comedic content, interesting points of view, and opportunities to go deep and give me a chance to chew on the content and formulate a response. If it's important to me, maybe it will be important to you as well. My thoughts, beliefs and words just might pack a wallop and be valuable to them.

My son, Russ, encouraged me to put my thoughts down on paper and create a piece that was uniquely *Rowgo*. I couldn't do it without a lot of help from my friends though. I took Facebook posts and expanded and expounded on them. That's where my "two cents" entered the mix.

Many of my loved ones have said that after I relocate to Heaven, they will hear my voice in their head. I thought about that a lot and started to get a little concerned. What if they heard it wrong or in a way different from how I meant it? I certainly didn't want anyone misconstruing, misunderstanding, or misinterpreting anything I said. Selective hearing is a thing, you know.

My solution seemed obvious, write it down in black and white. People will often read into what is written any way they choose. Shoot, they've been doing it for years. Very scholarly tomes—even the Bible—have been scrutinized and criticized by thousands upon thousands of people. But the people who know me well, and for whom *Two Cents* was written, will read it, hear my voice, and know exactly what I meant.

Here's the bottom line: Facebook fed me posts evoking comments from me. I wrote what rose up in my spirit. I am fully convinced that God inspired me to write what appears on the pages of *Two Cents*. It has been written with the following sections: Focused Inward (self), Focused Outward (others), and Focused Upward (God). As you make your way through the book, you will discover that although these sections help to direct our actions, all three of these focal areas are inextricably intertwined.

My motivation was to leave a bit of what mattered the most to me behind for the family and friends who mattered the most to me. These are the people who loved and encouraged me to become who I was created to be. There might even be a possibility that some I've never met before will come across *Two Cents*. To you I say "Welcome!" And to keep this conversation alive, I've also left room for you to include your comments. "A penny for your thoughts," so to speak. Perhaps by the time you've read through this book, you'll feel like you already know me as well. It's so nice to have met you. I hope you enjoyed every minute of our time together!

Blessings!

1

FOCUSED INWARD

IN THE BLINK OF AN EYE

In the blink of an eye, everything can change…
so, forgive often and love with all your heart.
You may never know when you may not have that chance.

Be mindful… everyone's days are numbered, but we don't know when our number will be called. Learn how to love well, be kind, and forgive often. Connect well and as frequently as busy schedules allow with family and friends—they are your people and your greatest gifts. They help to give your life meaning. Be teachable and learn from the One who placed you here in the first place. God has a wonderful plan for your life.

Live each moment with purpose, and make every day count. Most importantly, live for Jesus! If I don't see you again this side of Glory, I'm hoping I haven't left anything important unsaid. Know that I love you and hope to see you later in that very special place where *all* the questions have been answered, and love and joy is eternal. Until then, live your best life and don't waste a moment. Life is an adventure!

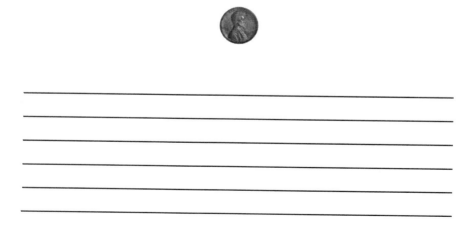

_____

_____

_____

_____

_____

POLITICAL & PANDEMIC PANDEMONIUM 2020

When Covid-19 hit, everybody seemed to have an opinion about what was true and what wasn't true. They voiced their opinions vociferously, creating great divisions within families, and many friendships fell by the wayside. This was addressed by my sweet friend and *bonus daughter*, MollyAnn Wymer Stinson, right when things were really starting to heat up.

Some of us sit and watch others spew pure ignorance on a variety of topics—forgetting that we too—are ignorant in some way about something. We are not required to have opinions on every topic. We cannot possibly know everything. What we see is often misleading, and so much is hidden that it can completely undo what we thought we knew once it is exposed.

I hold my tongue and my fingers from the keyboard... a lot. Many of us do. There are a few things I can speak confidently on. It is a very short list. But it's a short list that has a fire burning under it. I am highly passionate about those few things, and, when I see or hear them tested with ignorance, it's like gasoline has been thrown on my internal fire.

So, I would encourage you—challenge you—during this time of "we all have an opinion" to stop having it for a while. Why DO you believe what you believe? What/who is the source of that belief?

I was once on the other side of those questions numb in my ignorance. Surely, my ignorance abounds in many areas still. Politics? Religion? What's actually going on? An elite percentage know for certain. The majority of us? We must recognize our inability to know fully what is created in the dark except through divine intervention and deep prayers for wisdom and discernment.

I saw a stranger on a friend's page say quite boastfully, "If you believe _____, we cannot be friends." I know for a fact the thing she spoke so adamantly against is one of my short list topics, and she was completely ignorant. My first reaction was to set her straight and flatten her from ever daring to speak with authority on the topic again... and there I saw my heart and my sin. I am that woman to someone else, somewhere when I have ranted from ignorance.

I can easily be most angered by those that I am the most like. Our mirror in human form tends to drive us to the madness of throwing rocks at the person before us, only to find it is our very image that angered us... what we saw in them that lies in us.

Let your short list be laid at the feet of Jesus. Lay your opinions and ideologies there and let His fire burn them and refine them in the light of truth.

Truth is a narrow pathway, and few find it. It should have all of us, myself included, on our faces and off of our ignorant tirades.

A lie, even spoken in ignorance, is still a lie. The truth told is always the truth told. Father, let my mouth be shut when I am ignorant; let me be a messenger of truth. Forgive me in my ignorance when I've seen myself as right in my own eyes. Even now, show me. In Jesus' name, Amen.

MollyAnn Wymer Stinson

March 22, 2020

Because You have been my help, therefore in the shadow of Your wings I will rejoice. My soul follows close behind You; Your right hand upholds me. But those who seek my life, to destroy it, shall go into the lower parts of the earth. They shall fall by the sword; they shall be a portion for jackals. But the king shall rejoice in God; Everyone who swears by Him shall glory; But the mouth of those who speak lies shall be stopped.
Psalm 63:7-11 (NKJV)

Oh, Molly... you've done it again! You have penned the ultimate challenge to all of us to hold our peace, look in the mirror to see the image reflected back at us, and thoughtfully consider the ways we choose to share our opinions—or rather—to hold our peace and pray. This gets to the core of the matter. *Brilliant!*

_____

_____

_____

_____

_____

_____

_____

_____

_____

_____

_____

_____

_____

_____

_____

_____

_____

_____

WASTED STRENGTH

God didn't give you the strength to get back on your feet so that you could run back to the same thing that knocked you down.

JCLU FOREVER

That would be insanity.
And yet it happens... all... the... time! *Stop it!*

_____

_____

_____

_____

_____

_____

_____

_____

_____

_____

_____

_____

_____

_____

_____

CEO STATUS

Evaluate the people in your life; then promote, demote, or terminate.
You're the CEO of your own life.

Make sure your people picker is firing on all cylinders and start doing a major tune-up. Life is too short and developing quality relationships will make your life ever so much more valuable and fulfilling.

_____

_____

_____

_____

_____

_____

_____

_____

_____

_____

_____

_____

_____

A WORTHY FIGHT

Obstacles are put in your way to see if what you want is really worth fighting for.

This falls into the category of "How bad do you want it?" Life is full of choices, and everyone has developed a list of priorities, good and not-so-good, whether they realize it or not. Giving up is always an option, but that's how opportunities are stifled and snuffed out. Never give up!

_____

_____

_____

_____

_____

_____

_____

_____

_____

_____

_____

_____

_____

_____

WHAT DO YOU THINK?

Some think that winning the Super Bowl, shooting a big elk, running a large corporation, or even becoming president of the United States are some of the greatest accomplishments and make someone great. But listen to the wisdom of God about what is great:

He that rules his own spirit is greater than he that takes a city...
Proverbs 16:32b

And listen to wisdom and truth from Jesus about who is great:

But he that is greatest among you shall be your servant...
Matthew 23:11

Some who have accomplished what most would consider to be great feats have not yet accomplished the greatest feats of all... governing their own lives. We celebrate, applaud, and admire those who we think have done Great Things. But if that same person is not able to govern their own life and does not serve others, they have not done the greatest things. Let's give ourselves today to what God reveals in the Word to be the Greater Things.

Guy Duininck

I've got my hands full taking care of myself—my physical, emotional, attitudinal, and spiritual self. On top of that, being a noticer of what's going on around me in my world gives me plenty to do to help when I'm able. It might never make the headlines, but it gives me purpose and that's enough. I live to please One in this season of my life. Hearing "Well done, good and faithful servant" is a worthy enough goal for me.

Stay calm; mind your own business; do your own job. You've
heard all this from us before, but a reminder never hurts.
1 Thessalonians 4:11 (MSG)

SHAKE OFF APATHY

Nothing results from apathy.

Max Lucado

Apathy is defined as a lack of interest, enthusiasm, or concern. There is no motivation to do anything about anything. When we show indifference and a lack of caring about what's going on around us, nothing changes. The "value" of complacency in God's eyes is summed up well in Revelations:

> **So, because you are lukewarm, and neither hot nor cold, I will spit you out of My mouth.**
> **Revelations 3:16 (ESV)**

As my dad used to say, "It's time to pee or get off the pot!" *Do something!* Apathy is a waste of the precious time we have been given to accomplish much in this life. Shake off apathy and start living a life that matters. You only live once!

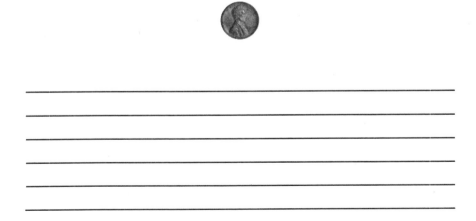

_____

_____

_____

_____

_____

_____

I'M NOT WRONG

If I'm wrong about God, then I wasted my life.

If you're wrong about God, then you wasted your life.

Lecrae

Even if I'm wrong about God—which I'm not (I fact checked)—I don't consider for a nanosecond that my life has been wasted. By following God's Word, I have loved well, learned to establish healthy boundaries, been a good steward with God's resources, and practiced generosity. My goal and joy in life has been to become all He created me to be, and that has not been a waste at all.

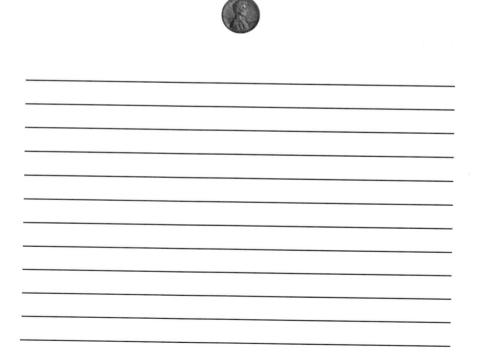

MY OWN BEST FRIEND

When a woman becomes her own best friend,

life is easier.

There's a lot to be said about being comfortable in your own skin. No matter where you go, there you are. When the self-bashing and negative self-talk ceases, real growth toward real maturity can commence! Who doesn't need a friend like that?

Additionally, there is one more point that needs to be made though. There is a Friend who will stick closer than a brother—or sister—or anybody for that matter. His name is Jesus! He defines you because He knows you better than you know yourself and please believe me when I say, *He is crazy about you!* He will teach you how to value, love, and embrace the person He says you are. What a friend you have in Jesus, and *that*, my friend, is how you become your own best friend.

DON'T SETTLE

Don't settle.

Either they will wake up to the fact that you are worth more...

or you will.

Charles Orlando

Who are you going to believe? Your own voice *or* the voices of many *or* the voice of the One who is responsible for giving you life in the first place? Gain wisdom, perspective, and insight—and believe God. He *knows* what He's talking about, and you *are* who He says you are. God says you are precious to Him, and He loves you. That ought to be worth something!

FEELINGS

Feelings are indicators, not dictators.

They can indicate where your heart is in the moment,

but that doesn't mean they have the right to boss you around.

You are more than the sum total of your feelings.

Lysa TerKeurst

This is so true. Too often feelings rule us. It's time for us to rule over our feelings. How many times have we heard "You're not the boss of me!" when facing conflict with someone? We can make the same declaration when dealing with our feelings too. Besides, feelings are fickle and only produce instability when they are allowed to run amok.

IN SESSION

It's a school of hard knocks for those who leave God's path,

a dead-end street for those who hate God's rules.

Proverbs 15:10 (MSG)

I have watched way too many people burn hot for Jesus for a season and then get distracted by the cares of the world and enticing temptations that lure them away from God's best plans for their lives.

Let's face it, none of us likes being told what to do. Often one of the first words out of our kid's mouth is "NO!" We often resent rules and look for ways to circumvent them, but the truth about rules is that they provide safety and—wait for it—*freedom!* Rules are boundaries for our welfare.

Boundaries, which originated with God, were His way of showing us kindness and helping us to become all we were created to be. We are certainly free to make our own choices and ignore God's boundaries, but there will be consequences when we get off track. God's favor, which I like to refer to as *Godwinks*, becomes very sparse when rebellion abounds. Keep an eye out for the warning signs posted along the path—and stay on track.

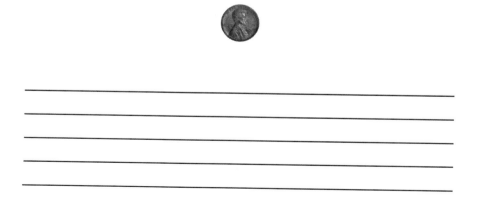

_____

_____

_____

_____

_____

SMART SHOPPERS

You know how you'll eat ANYTHING when you're starving?
Like you'll go to the grocery store on an empty stomach and just come home
with weird stuff you don't need? Yeah. Don't go out into the world with an
empty soul. You'll fill up on all kinds of crap. Be sure to nourish yourself FIRST.

Nanea Hoffman

We have been told to never go grocery shopping on an empty stomach. Invariably, we overspend and come home with way more stuff than we have room to store away. We wind up with food that isn't good for us or even wanted after some time, so it eventually gets tossed out. Why not be more judicious and smarter in the first place? Being lonely and feeling empty often leads to shopping and settling for anything and anyone. If we will take the time and load up on the bare necessities at home, like being full of ourselves (but in a healthy way), we are more likely to be able to pick and choose what is truly good for us.

We would be especially wise if we asked God to fill our cup and satisfy our souls with everything we need as a single person. He has promised to do that. Then, trusting His guidance, we will be able to go out and "shop" well for the people who will truly satisfy our souls.

_____

_____

_____

I AM A BROKEN RECORD

Boundaries are the only mechanism for keeping the bad stuff out and the good stuff in. If you want to overcome discouragement, boundaries are vital.

Andy Andrews

I know that I sound like a broken record—and many millennials won't even know what I mean by using the word "record"—but here's a fact-checked truth:

Boundaries are absolutely essential to be safe *and* to enjoy freedom.

Sometimes we become discouraged because we know that we aren't living our best life and we don't know why or what to do about it. Maybe I can expand on Andy's statement and suggest that maybe, just maybe, there's some bad stuff that has taken up residence within our boundaries. If that's the case, since we are the gatekeepers of our own boundaries, there is nothing stopping us from removing the toxic, bad stuff. We can swing the gate open, kick it out, and banish it forever. We have control over what we allow in and what we keep out. That is safety, protection, peace, and freedom in a nutshell—and it eliminates discouragement.

_____

_____

_____

MAYDAY! MAYDAY!

Ships don't sink because of the water around them. Ships sink because of the water that gets in them. Don't let what's happening around you get inside you and weigh you down.

B e your own gatekeeper. Don't allow anyone without a ticket to board your ship. Exercise strong boundaries that will ensure your safety. Storms will always be swirling, and chaos is present in the world today. If you guard against entering into the fray and don't let the troubles penetrate and affect your life, you will stay afloat and survive.

_____

_____

_____

_____

_____

_____

_____

_____

_____

When you're in over your head, I'll be there with you. When you're in rough waters, you will not go down.
Isaiah 43:2a (MSG)

BALANCE

I used to think I was introverted because I enjoyed being alone, but it turns out I really liked being at peace with myself and my surroundings... and I am extremely extroverted with people who bring me comfort and happiness.

The operative word is *balance*. Experiencing peace and being comfortable living in my own skin and in my own company is great, but I also realize that God has not called me to live my life in isolation. The balancing act involves finding wonderful, safe friends who can fill up my love tank while I return the favor. We can gather together for fun and laughter... and yes, even tears, while talking about life and things that matter to us. I think this has been God's plan all along.

My friend, Christina, added a powerful comment to this post. "Balance is right. Alone time with God gives us wisdom and confidence so that we crave healthy relationship circles. The right social environments bring us introverts alive with zest and generosity."

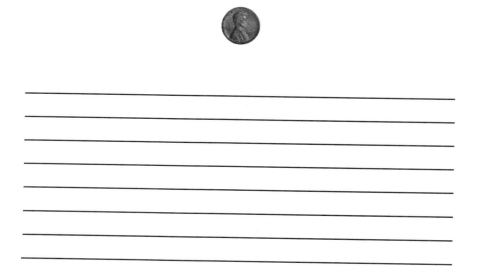

_____

_____

_____

_____

_____

_____

_____

CARROTS, EGGS, OR COFFEE?

Dedicated to my grandchildren

A young woman went to her grandmother and told her about her life and how things were so hard for her. She did not know how she was going to make it and wanted to give up. She was tired of fighting and struggling. It seemed as one problem was solved, a new one arose.

Her grandmother took her to the kitchen. She filled three pots with water. In the first, she placed carrots, in the second she placed eggs, and in the last she placed ground coffee beans. She let them sit and boil without saying a word.

In about 20 minutes, she turned off the burners. She fished the carrots out and placed them in a bowl. She pulled the eggs out and placed them in a bowl. Then she ladled the coffee out and placed it in a bowl. Turning to her granddaughter, she asked, "Tell me... what do you see?"

"Carrots, eggs, and coffee," she replied.

She brought her closer and asked her to feel the carrots. She did and noted that they got soft. She then asked her to take an egg and break it. After pulling off the shell, she observed the hard-boiled egg.

Finally, she asked her to sip the coffee. The granddaughter smiled as she tasted its rich aroma. The granddaughter then asked, "What's the point, Grandmother?"

Her grandmother explained that each of these objects had faced the same adversity—boiling water—but each reacted differently.

The carrot went in strong, hard, and unrelenting. However, after being subjected to the boiling water, it softened and became weak. The egg had been fragile. Its thin outer shell had protected its liquid interior. But, after sitting through the boiling water, its inside became hardened.

The ground coffee beans were unique, however. After they were in the boiling water, they had changed the water.

"Which are you?" she asked her granddaughter. "When adversity knocks on your door, how do you respond? Are you a carrot, an egg, or a ground coffee bean?"

Think of this: Which am I?

Am I the carrot that seems strong, but with pain and adversity, do I wilt and become soft and lose my strength?

Am I the egg that starts with a malleable heart, but changes with the heat? Did I have a fluid spirit, but after a death, a breakup, a financial hardship, or some other trial, have I become hardened and stiff? Does my shell look the same, but on the inside am I bitter and tough with a stiff spirit and a hardened heart?

Or am I like the coffee bean? The bean actually changes the hot water, the very circumstance that brings the pain. When the water gets hot, it releases the fragrance and flavor. If you are like the bean, when things are at their worst, you get better and change the situation around you.

When the hours are the darkest and trials are their greatest, do you elevate to another level?

AUTHOR UNKNOWN

_____

_____

_____

_____

_____

_____

_____

_____

_____

_____

_____

_____

JOY TRUMPS HAPPINESS

People who have happiness as their goal get locked into the pain/pleasure motivation cycle. They never do what causes them pain, but always do what brings them pleasure. This puts us on the same thinking level as a child who has difficulty seeing past his or her fear of pain and love of pleasure.

Dr. John Townsend

The Entitlement Cure

My grandson, Steve, and I had quite a conversation in the summer of 2019 about the contrast between happiness and joyfulness. We agreed that so many people just want to be happy, as if that is their ultimate goal in life. But is that enough? Happiness can be so fleeting. Could there be a higher order to shoot for in this life?

Happiness is a rather fundamental feeling and is usually experienced and enjoyed due to external circumstances or the presence of people who bring special meaning or emotional highs into our life. It ebbs and flows on how well things and relationships are going on around us. It lacks predictable stability though—it's shaky.

Joy, on the other hand, operates at a higher and out of a much deeper level. It tends to be an inside out phenomenon that sometimes begins to bubble up out of nowhere. It's kind of like an artesian well that doesn't require any effort or pumping up. It just is! There's a sense, though a bit irrational, that everything is well with the world, even though upon looking around, it's easy to see that it isn't. And yet... joy remains.

As I shared with Steve, I was able to convey to him how special God had been in my life. Just thinking about all the wonderful things He has done at the most unexpected times throughout my life quickens a rising of an inexplicable joy from down deep in the center of my very being. It often moves me to tears of great gratitude. There are no words at times like that. Joy unspeakable and full of glory trumps fickle happiness by a long shot. Happiness or joy... they aren't the same. Go for joy!

If Steve ever reads this, I want him to recall the time he sat at the kitchen table eating tomato soup and a grilled cheese sandwich in the company of the woman he loved with his whole heart. It wasn't a glamorous scene with high-end cuisine, but he was enJOYing a fine conversation with his special person. He told me later that the joy was bubbling out of nowhere, and it felt great and so special. Not very much time passed before there was a wedding. Steve and Amanda got married. Now *that* was a *joyful* occasion!

BAD MEDS

Don't try to medicate dysfunction with spending.
No amount of stuff will get rid of pain or make you happy.

Dave Ramsey

When things are not going well and thinking gets screwed up, it's easy to think that a shopping spree will make things all better. That kind of solution is dysfunctional on top of an already dysfunctional lifestyle. I can remember when a family member charged a boom box over 25 years ago. By the time the overloaded credit card was paid off, the boom box had been trashed. They were still paying for stuff that no longer had purpose or value. No happiness there except that the card was finally paid off. Financial responsibility and good stewardship can put a happy smile on anyone's face.

_____

_____

_____

_____

_____

_____

_____

_____

_____

WHAT IS AN ASKHOLE?

An askhole is a person who constantly asks for your advice,
but always does the opposite of what you tell them.

I didn't coin this word—wish I had—but I've used it frequently. So many times, I have been approached by people, either in therapy/counseling sessions or just in everyday settings and have been asked for direction or advice. Being a people person, I try to be generous with my time. Admittedly, I don't know everything by a long shot, but I'm happy to share what I do know with anyone who asks. If the questions are in the area of my study and expertise, I will pass on "words of wisdom," strategies on how to get out of situations or toxic relationships, how to be a good steward with money and how to budget, how to implement God's plan for a better life, how to practice humility and resolve family problems, how to be a safe person and build quality relationships, and how to establish healthy boundaries. These are the main areas I can address confidently—relationship stuff with God and others. I am also at the ready to offer my two cents on other things as well, when asked.

It's so disheartening when an inordinate amount of time is given to someone, and I know that what I've said is good and has merit, and yet that person will go off and do the same nonsense over and over again. Insanity, right? When they come back later—sometimes much later—and nothing has changed and maybe even gotten worse, I try not to sigh and roll my eyes. I sure don't say, "Really? I'm so sorry. What can I do to help?" These days I ask if they have done what I told them to do last time we spent hours "solving" their problems. The answer is usually "No" or "I tried it (for a minute) and it didn't work."

SPECIAL NOTE HERE: We do this with God, don't we? We all have been askholes at one time or another.

I have learned that all I can do is share what I know that would or could help. Then the ball is in their court to let it fly right past them and over their head, or they can connect with it and make it go where it needs to go. Not my problem, and I can't make anybody do anything, even if it's the right thing to do. I will live my life, share when asked, and not bust anybody's boundary by insisting that they do anything they're not ready or willing to do. I won't lie though; it does create a level of frustration in me when people refuse to respond well to wise counsel. I eventually get over it. God is well able to carry on from there.

DO THE RIGHT THING

WRONG IS WRONG

Even if everyone is doing it.

RIGHT IS RIGHT

Even if no one is doing it.

Here's a very strong word from two versions of the Bible found in James to address this straightforward statement.

But now you boast in your arrogance. All such boasting is evil. Therefore, to him who knows to do good and does not do it, to him it is sin.
James 4:16-17 (NKJV)

As it is, you are full of your grandiose selves. All such vaunting self-importance is evil. In fact, if you know the right thing to do and don't do it, that, for you, is evil.
James 4:16-17 (MSG)

Christian, if you ever say, "I probably shouldn't feel, think, say, or do this, *but___*," you need to silence the *but* and stop right there in your tracks. *You know!* Your gut or conscience or whatever is sounding a warning. Let's face it, that niggling sense that is creating your uneasiness and saying, "Don't go there. Don't do it" is the Holy Spirit, your Helper, reminding you that you *do* know better. *And if you know better, do better!*

**Therefore, you shall be careful to do as the Lord your God
has commanded you; you shall not turn aside to the right or
to the left. You shall walk in all the ways which the Lord
Your God has commanded you, that you may live and that it
may be well with you, and that you may prolong your days
in the land which you shall possess.
Deuteronomy 5:32-33 (NKJV)**

CHECK YOUR OWN BAGGAGE

Note to self:

Good news about those big heavy suitcases full of other people's opinions and judgments and misconceptions you've been lugging around all over town. You can just set those down and walk away.

They're not yours; they never were.

Nanea Hoffman

What's yours is yours. Own it! What belongs to others—their opinions and judgments and misconceptions about you—is NOT your concern. Leave it alone! If you pick it up and allow it to disturb your peace, those people have successfully busted your boundaries, and you let them. Check the tags on the suitcases and only pick up what has your name on it.

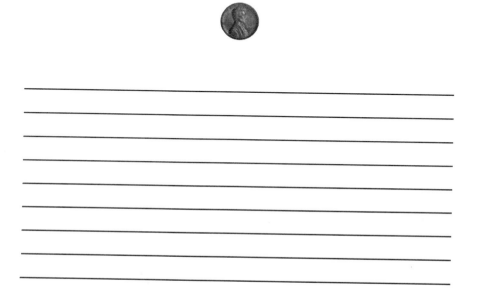

KNOW THE DIFFERENCE

Love didn't hurt you.

Someone who doesn't know how to love... hurt you.

Don't confuse the two.

Trent Shelton

G ood distinction! I'll bet a lot of people have thought about the song *I Wanna Know What Love Is* after experiencing the end of a traumatic, toxic, hurtful relationship. They thought they knew but simply didn't.

God is perfect love and loves perfectly; people don't. Maybe if we took the time to bask in God's love and developed a deep, meaningful relationship with Him, we would be able to identify and connect with people who exhibit the same loving character traits.

There is absolutely nothing wrong with love, but we've got to *know* what it is. Many people think they know and use the word all the time, but many times the word has lost its value in errant translations. People need to sort out the true meaning of love. *Hint: The Bible contains the best definition. Check out I Corinthians 13 for starters... and go from there.*

I really believe people want to genuinely love that special someone, and they will profusely profess their love often, but when that "love" is tangled up with so many things that are lacking real love, the fault is in not having a clear and concise knowledge of what real love looks like. Look to the Master. He will teach all of us who are willing to learn

_____

_____

_____

_____

_____

_____

_____

_____

_____

_____

_____

_____

_____

_____

_____

_____

_____

_____

Love suffers long and is kind; love does not envy; love does
not parade itself, is not puffed up; does not behave rudely,
does not seek its own, is not provoked, thinks no evil; does
not rejoice in iniquity, but rejoices in the truth; bears all
things, believes all things, hopes all things, endures all
things. Love never fails.
I Corinthians 13:4-8b (NKJV)

TIME MANAGEMENT

Quit saying you don't have time.
You have time for what you make time for in your life.

Bryant McGill

We can manage to make time for what really matters, but we must prioritize. When the moment passes without acting on the thought or action, we can't get it back. We need to live life like we mean it. Make it count for something that matters. Even small acts have eternal consequences.

_____

_____

_____

_____

_____

_____

_____

_____

_____

_____

_____

_____

GONE WITH THE WIND

Sometimes I wish I could press 'Record' for when what comes out of my mouth has the occational flash of brilliant wisdom and insight in the speaking. When asked to say it again, it's gone with the wind.

Rowgo

I can remember back to the time that I used to lead groups. Occasionally, I would speak about something pertinent to what we were learning, and a group member would ask me if I could repeat it. The answer was always the same... *nope*. The flash of inspiration would be gone. I could remember the gist of what was said, but not the exact wording. Am I the only one who does this?

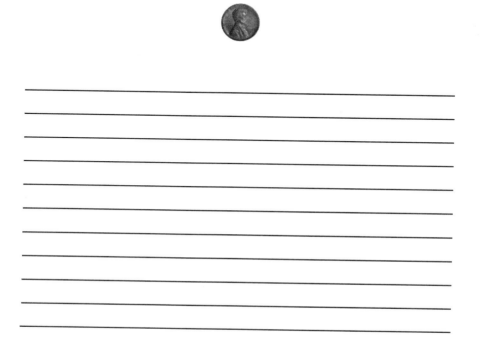

_____

_____

_____

_____

_____

_____

_____

_____

_____

_____

ERASERS

An old man said, "Erasers are made for those who make mistakes.

A youth replied, "Erasers are made for those who are willing to correct their mistakes!"

Attitude matters.

Perspective matters too. It's easy to wipe out a mistake and make it appear to disappear. Out of sight; out of mind—right? However, more might be required and necessary. If a mistake has been made and needs to be corrected with visible results, it might be time to flip over the eraser and make the correction. Make a point of giving attention to the problem areas and correcting the mistakes.

FILL YOUR CUP

Yesterday I was clever, so, I wanted to change the world.
Today I am wise, so, I am changing myself.

I t's all about knowing where to begin. You can't pour from an empty cup. Every day lived is an opportunity to learn new things and gain fresh perspectives and Godly wisdom. As this begins to happen, your ability to make a difference in the world increases. More importantly, personal changes begin to become more apparent to those around you as you are able to pour from a full cup.

JUST WALK AWAY

Walk away from people who put you down.

Walk away from fights that will never be resolved.

Walk away from trying to please people who will never see your worth.

The more you walk away from things that poison your soul,

the healthier you will be.

Walking is good for your health. As you walk away from where you've been, it's important to set a new destination. Keep your eyes on the finish line and don't turn back.

_____

_____

_____

_____

_____

_____

_____

_____

_____

_____

_____

CLICK POWER

One day it just clicks.

You realize what's important and what isn't.

You learn to care less about what other people think of you and more about what you think of yourself. You realize how far you've come and you remember when you thought things were such a mess that you would never recover. And you smile. You smile because you are truly proud of yourself and the person you've fought to become.

tinybuddha.com

What's that I hear? Why, it's a whole bunch of clicking. Now *that* puts a smile on my face! Self-care is an incredibly powerful and worthy endeavor. A testimony like this is such an encouragement to others who are struggling.

BREAKTHROUGH BLOCKERS

The only thing you can control 100% of the time is your attitude.

Joel Osteen

This is a good thing to remember while waiting for a breakthrough. An attitude develops in the mind and heart and proceeds to come out of the mouth and in behaviors. Don't put up a wall, blocking your breakthrough by exhibiting a crummy attitude.

_____

_____

_____

_____

_____

_____

_____

_____

_____

_____

_____

_____

_____

_____

_____

WHAT IS THE (REAL) QUESTION?

The following concept has eaten at the souls of everyone throughout all time. Knowing the answer to this question is a central need and is of overwhelming importance. It drives the motivations and the hesitations of every individual, whether consciously or not.

"Who am I?"

The quick answer is to equate how we see ourselves with simply the known reality of our situation. If we are all we see and the environment we find ourselves in is nothing more than what our five senses reveal to us, the answer is simple - "I am a unique, physical presence, born into existence through purely physical means. Full of thoughts and emotions sure, but I am only what I am. My purpose is what I choose it to be."

I can be selfish or helpful – brutal or gracious – destructive or uplifting. I can even be all the above when that "me" suits me. You know, I can pretty much do anything or be anything I want. Nothing I do would ever conflict with my interpretation of "Who I Am." After all, who is to say who I need to be – except me?

If that is you, there is something that requires consideration. The answer to the question you seek demands perspective—one that many people refuse to consider.

A young infant may look in a mirror and be convinced there is another child *in there*. Every neuron of knowledge that infant is using can never allow the truth to be revealed. Place a mirror before an animal and watch them seek to attack the competitor in the "window" in a useless effort of bravado. In fact, the more emotionally driven the effort, the more difficult it is to convince that the threat is baseless.

Perhaps we are looking at ourselves with the wrong mirror.

What if you are not the central theme of the question at all? What if the question isn't about you? What if the question is really about the Central Theme which, because of your pure physical nature and understanding, you simply cannot see? I venture that no one can see – *IT* – unless they can consider the bigger question. This is the question that, once understood, will answer the first question.

"Whose am I?"

Rusty James

My answer is simple, definitive, and final. I belong to the One who created me and loves me unconditionally, no holds barred.

HARDSHIPS

Hardships often prepare ordinary people for an extraordinary destiny.

C.S. Lewis

We don't like hardships; they aren't pleasant. Sometimes it seems as if there is no way out, but there it is. There are a couple of options: Wallow in it and stay stuck *or* see it as an opportunity and challenge to do something about it. Paint over the canvas and change the picture. The results will be an extraordinary masterpiece!

WHOSE MESS IS IT?

Don't blame your behavior on someone else. You are 100% responsible no matter how bad you are feeling or what's happening in your life.

Do something about it. Nobody else needs to do it for you—nor can they—it's not their job! There isn't one single person on this planet who hasn't been given a life assignment, but it is exclusively *their* assignment. They will be busy enough taking care of their own business without stepping into your mess. If they were to step in and do your assignment, they would be busting your boundary—even if you never developed one and it was invisible.

If you don't have a clue and lack the life skills to resolve your predicament, by all means, get help—the right kind of help. But here's the bottom line. Others may give instruction and show you how to get the job done, but, in the end, it's still your responsibility to do it.

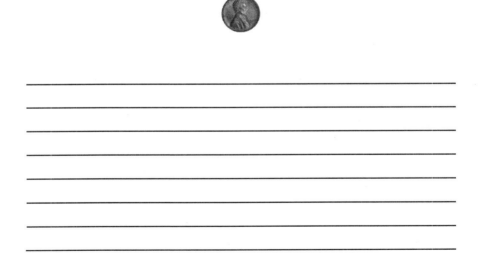

_____

_____

_____

_____

_____

_____

_____

STAY IN YOUR OWN LANE

Let go of people who dull your shine, poison your spirit, and bring you drama.
Cancel your subscription to their issues.

Quotes 'n Thoughts

Everyone has issues of their own to navigate and manage. Stay in your own lane! It's easy to be misled and get off track when you're around all kinds of people, so be vigilant. I Corinthians sounds the warning:

Do not be deceived: Evil company corrupts good habits.
I Corinthians 15:33 (NKJV)

When you subscribe to anything, make sure it will be beneficial and add quality to your life. If it doesn't, you can't afford a subscription like that.

_____

_____

_____

_____

_____

_____

_____

_____

_____

STUPIDITY

Definition of stupidity:
Knowing the truth,
seeing the evidence of the truth,
but still believing the lies.

This reminds me of Lee Strobel, the author of *The Case For Christ*, a book which was also adapted into a movie. Check it out. Lee corrected his wrong thinking and belief system by systematically setting out to prove the death and resurrection of Christ never happened.

He put in long hours doing the research, interviewing knowledgeable scientists, and studying hard to prove it was hogwash and people were stupid to believe such nonsense, only to discover that all evidence supported that it *did* happen—just like the Bible said. He had been wrong all along, even though he felt 100% confident that he had been right in his thinking.

Lee did the right and the smart thing though and changed his mind and wrong thinking. He was transformed by the renewal of his mind. Consequently, this transformation changed his life for the better when he embraced this truth.

Therefore, I urge you, brothers and sisters, in view of God's mercy, to offer your bodies as a living sacrifice, holy and pleasing to God—this is your true and proper worship. Do not conform to the pattern of this world, but be transformed by the renewing of your mind. Then you will be able to test and approve what God's will is—his good, pleasing and perfect will.
Romans 12:1,2 (NIV)

_____

_____

_____

_____

_____

_____

_____

_____

_____

_____

_____

_____

_____

_____

_____

_____

_____

_____

Every part of Scripture is God-breathed and useful one way
or another---showing us truth, exposing our rebellion,
correcting our mistakes, training us to live God's way.
Through the Word we are put together and shaped up for
the tasks God has for us.
II Timothy 3:16-17 (MSG)

BACKWARD AND UPSIDE-DOWN

There are people who don't let what the Word of God says get in the way of what they believe.

Andrew Wommack

This is a profound statement, and I have adopted—and even adapted—it many times. It is so backward and upside-down. No wonder there are so many people living less-than-victorious lives. Distorted thinking, unrenewed minds, and screwed-up beliefs have gotten in the way and short-circuited successful living.

I'm thinking back on an old Peter, Paul and Mary song, *Where Have All the Flowers Gone?* The final line is: "When will they ever learn? When will they ever learn?" This song was an anti-war song back in the day, but it has a much bigger meaning for me. When will we ever learn that there is only one God—and we are *not* Him! We'd *better* get off the throne and let the Word of God get in the way of what *we* believe, or we will be suffering the consequences of our arrogance and pride. It's time to think and believe right—so that we can live right!

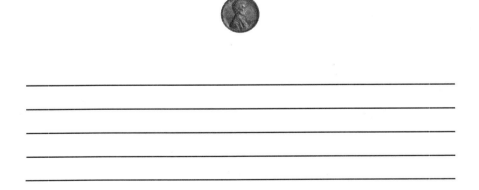

I DON'T FEEL LIKE IT

The worst battle you have to fight is between what you know and what you feel.

Wisdom Quotes

When I was a child and my mom told me to do something, on occasion I would get sassy and say, "But I don't feel like it!" No matter what "it" was, I would get oppositional and refuse to do what she wanted me to do, because I didn't feel like it. She would say, "Do it anyway." If I felt brave enough to push the envelope, I would belligerently ask why I had to do what she asked. She didn't very often say, "Because I said so." That response from a parent has always infuriated kids around the world. My mom, in her great wisdom, would very calmly answer my question with, "Because it's the right thing to do, and you *know* it."

It is prudent to lean toward the side of what we know is the right thing to do rather than yielding to fickle feelings.

_____

_____

_____

_____

_____

_____

_____

DO THE HARD THINGS

One of the hardest things to do in life is letting go of what you thought was real.

Often what we think in our mind is real turns out to be a picture of our ideal life. We operate somewhere between reality and what we are striving to achieve in life... our picture of what an ideal life looks like. We will never quite make it this side of Heaven, but it's a worthy goal and we can go for it. We won't be sorry in the long run, so there are no regrets. Just remember though, we aren't always the greatest at assessing what's really going on and what's real, for real. Don't white-knuckle it as you try to hang on to stuff that lacks authenticity. Let it go, so you can free up the death grip and be free to adjust and go after whatever makes more sense—*that which is real*.

_____
_____
_____
_____
_____
_____
_____
_____
_____
_____

THOUGHTS ARE A ROAD MAP

Be very careful about what you think...
your thoughts run your life.

How often does the Bible address this truth? It's all over the place, so it must be important. Proverbs 23:7 says: As a man thinks in his heart, so is he. Creflo Dollar has suggested moving the comma and reading it like this: As a man thinks, in his heart so is he.

Either way, whatever we focus our thoughts on the most tends to create the impulse to act and directs how we go about exercising that action. It is wisdom and advantageous to govern the way we think, because our thoughts will ultimately determine our actions and how well we live our lives. If we learn how to think the way that God thinks, we won't be sorry. Our actions will be righteous and altogether the best way to go.

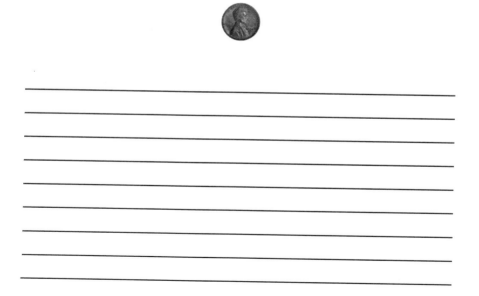

_____

_____

_____

_____

_____

_____

_____

_____

_____

EVERYBODY MATTERS

Your Impact on other people is bigger than you think.

Someone still giggles when they think of that funny thing you said.

Someone still smiles when they think of the compliment you gave them.

Someone silently admires you.

The advice you give has made a difference for people.

The support and love you've offered others has made someone's day.

Your input and opinions have made someone think twice.

You're not insignificant and forgotten.

Your existence makes a positive difference, whether you see it or not.

Compassionate Reminders

D o I want to make a difference? Well… yeah! Who doesn't? Wouldn't it be nice to hear from the people I have met over time that my presence in their lives made a difference? What I believe about my significance to others is sometimes just that—a belief—or maybe a hope. The only way I'll know for sure is if I'm fortunate enough to have the type of people in my life who are generous enough to say so.

And yet, if this is the kind of thing I'd love to hear from my family and friends, I might want to consider doing "the big reversal" and let them know all about the positive impact they have made in my life. I have certainly been greatly impacted by others and by every one of the things mentioned in this post. For that, I have been so blessed by the very special people who have crossed my path in this life. Accept my sincere thanks for adding so much vibrant color and beauty to my life. And, for whatever time I have left here and as often as is possible, I will try to make a point of letting everyone know up close and personal how much I love and appreciate them.

Love one another with brotherly affection. Outdo one
another in showing honor.
Romans 12:10 (NIV)

BARELY WADING

Any relationship you have that could get ruined by having a conversation about your feelings, standards, and/or expectations wasn't really stable enough to begin with.

tinybuddha.com

There is no depth at all in a relationship like this. Feelings, standards, and expectations should never be off limits. For any relationship to have real substance and work well, *both* parties must be willing to dive in and go deep. This requires a level of vulnerability and helps to build trust and authenticity. Anyone who is unwilling to discuss the deeper things of life will be wanting or settling for a very shallow connection. And the person who puts up with someone who won't talk about things that matter will wind up in the same boat. A relationship like that, if you can even call it that, has very little chance at a happily ever after.

_____

_____

_____

_____

_____

_____

_____

_____

BIG DIFFERENCE

Addiction is

giving up *everything* for one thing.

Recovery is

giving up one thing for *everything*.

My grandson, Steve, told me that recovery is hard work, and it isn't just about quitting the addiction, whatever it is. It can be alcohol, drugs, gambling, pornography, sexual behaviors. It can even be shopping so much that debt threatens bankruptcy, energy drinks, smoking, or anything that has an inordinate power and control over an individual. You get it! The list can go on and on. Steve said submitting to a legitimate, tested, and regulated recovery program is key, because it involves much more than a white-knuckle approach of vowing to stop the addictive behavior. There is a plan presented in the program and accountability to a sponsor or mentor who tracks the progress being made. The idea isn't to focus on stopping the addictive behaviors, but rather on the benefits and joys that a life without addictions can bring. It's not escaping from something; it's moving toward something and learning to develop the life skills needed to live a full life with purpose and joy.

Living an addictive lifestyle is very time-consuming, and when someone moves away from their addiction, a big hole is left that needs to be filled. So now what? With a big, gaping empty space, so often people get busy with work, kids, paying bills, and all kinds of activities to fill up that big hole. Here's the problem: all the busy-ness involves frenetic external activities, but the hole is internal and needs a special kind of attention. *That* needs to be cleaned out, healed, and filled from the inside out.

Steve said the hardest step in the 12-Step Program for many is the first step, *surrender*. But to gain back everything that has been lost, everyone needs help in the form of a support team of skilled, caring, and loving people. Success cannot be found in isolation. Most crucial is the decision to totally surrender to God willingly. It takes humility and the realization that He has the answers and the love and acceptance to bring full restoration and freedom from any and every addiction known to man.

PERSONAL DISCLOSURE: I have a major "addiction," and it began 50 years ago. It involved a major act of surrender! I fell in love with God—hook, line, and sinker. There's no turning back. This is one "addiction" that has served me well and my real friends encourage me to pursue this passion with everything I have so I can learn more and grow. If anyone wants to fill up that big hole that resulted from leaving a destructive lifestyle or a harmful addiction, filling that hole with the Lord brings fullness of life.

OVERWHELMED

I'm basking in God's goodness today...
IT IS OVERWHELMING!!!

Rowgo

I'd like to say this is an everyday occurrence, but—to be honest—some days I get caught up in stuff and concerns of what's going on around me. When I remember to stay in the eye of the storm, there is calm, and perfect peace, and *my* eye is stayed on Him. When I stick my toe out and into the chaos that is swirling around me, I am swept away into the turmoil. But today, I choose to be still and bask in God's goodness, remembering that He is good *all* the time. I am overwhelmed by that reality.

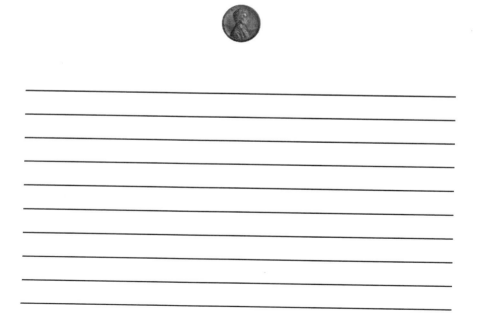

THE CIRCLE OF LIFE

Life is a circle of happiness, sadness, hard times, and good times.
If you are going through hard times, have faith that good times are on the way.

This describes the circle of life very well. Psalm 30:5 offers the rainbow and hope for the future: Weeping may last for a night, but joy comes in the morning. Nobody will ever escape this life without experiencing hard times, pain, and sadness, but choosing to live a life of faith in God is the assurance that "good times *are* on the way"—both here and in our final destination.

THINK AGAIN

Beware of those whose faith is based on their own ideas, feelings, and what they think is right... rather than on what God's Word says!

We all know people who won't let what the Bible says get in the way of what they think or feel. There's a four-letter word that describes these folks, and it's peppered throughout Proverbs. Oh, and it starts with the sixth letter of the alphabet. The word is *fool*... don't be one!

GETTING CREATIVE

When I get old, they're never going to say,

"What a sweet old lady."

They're gonna say,

"What on EARTH is she up to now?"

The more I realize that every day I live is one day closer to relocating to Heaven, the more excited I get about what else I can get done here before taking off. I don't want to leave any stone unturned or leave anything important unsaid. At this stage of my life, I've been super energized to do a few things I always wanted to do, but at times lacking the gumption to get off my duff and do them.

I'm not talking about physical stuff though; the body has slowed down. I can't do a lot of the things I used to do when I was younger—and I did a lot. But at least I still jog every morning... to the john. It's been said by others that they changed the name of their bathroom from john to jim. I decided to join that club. I go to the jim every day... frequently.

Even pushing Level 78, I am living my best life! The creative juices are flowing, and the ideas are forming and coming to fruition. Finally, at long last, I am doing something I've wanted to do for years, *I'm writing!* That's not to say that I've never written before. I've run across quite a few of the papers that I wrote back in my college days. I've held on to them for one reason or another. Each time I read them, there is something in them that suggests that I found value in putting my thoughts down on paper. Word usage has always been important to me; I am intrigued by the way words can be used to bring images and ideas to life. In the past, my son has referred to me as a wordsmith, and I have taken that as a compliment. At any rate, before very long, there might actually be a book. *That* is what I have been doing in my spare time. Who knows? You might even be reading this page in my long-time-coming book. God has been so very kind and good to me as He has encouraged me to pursue my interests. Life is such an adventure!

DENIAL

More people would learn from their mistakes if they weren't so busy denying them.

Zig Ziglar

Denial sure does get in the way of making positive life changes. Lots of folks are stuck and spinning their wheels and cannot imagine why they aren't enjoying the wonderful things life has to offer.

_____
_____
_____
_____
_____
_____
_____
_____
_____
_____
_____
_____
_____
_____
_____
_____

DECEPTIVE HEARTS

My heart isn't deceptive because it fools other people...
it's deceptive because it fools me.

Todd Staal

I can't go with my feelings, my gut, or what I believe to be true with my whole heart. Jeremiah 17:9 says the heart is deceitful. Even my own very best efforts are going to fall short at times. I need to be fully dependent on and agree with what God has to say about everything—period.

> **The heart is hopelessly dark and deceitful, a puzzle that no one can figure out. But I, God, search the heart and examine the mind. I get to the heart of the human. I get to the root of things. I treat them as they really are, not as they pretend to be.**
> **Jeremiah 17:9-10 (MSG)**

_____

_____

_____

_____

_____

_____

_____

HOW TO WRITE GOOD

Avoid alliteration. Always.

Prepositions are not words to end sentences with.

Avoid cliches like the plague. They're old hat.

Comparisons are as bad as cliches.

Be more or less specific.

Writers should never generalize.

Exaggeration is a billion times worse than understatement!

Don't be redundant; don't use more words than necessary, it's highly superfluous.

Who needs rhetorical questions?

Ten. Be Consistent!

I always—and I mean always— try to be more or less pacific when I write. And I eschew redundancy at all costs as well as trying desperately not to use too much unnecessary and fruitless verbiage. Writing good is what I live for. If I've said it once, I've said it a million times... who needs to bother with bad writing anyway?

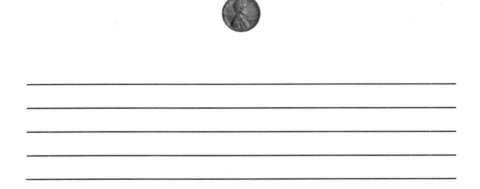

_____

_____

_____

_____

_____

SENSIBLE STABILITY

When we know something is bad for us,

we need to put our emotions aside and use our sensibility.

Don't stay in an unhealthy relationship just to avoid being alone.

There are plenty of filling stations where your love tank can get topped off in a very healthy way. That allows you the freedom to be comfortable in your own skin and actually enjoy your own company during alone times.

PROPER PERSPECTIVE

An Atheist's View on Life

I will live my life according to these beliefs

God does not exist

It is just foolish to think

That there is a God with a cosmic plan

That an all-powerful God brings redemption and healing to the pain and suffering in the world

Is a comforting thought, however,

It

Is only wishful thinking

People can do as they please without eternal consequences

The idea that

I am deserving of Hell

Because of sin

Is a lie meant to make me a slave to those in power

"The more you have, the happier you will be"

Our existence has no grand meaning or purpose

In a world with no God

There is freedom to be who I want to be

But with God

Everything is fine

It is ridiculous to think

I am lost and in need of saving

A Christian's View on Life

Now read this from the bottom to the top

This is genius. To think that one Man, Jesus, was the beginning of Christianity by turning the world upside-down with His Message. In my opinion, there is no better way to put this in proper perspective.

A HUGE PROBLEM

I have no problem with the Gospel being explained.

I have a HUGE problem with it being changed

in order not to offend anyone.

I Peter 2:6-8 says that the disobedient will be offended by the Word. *Oh well!* Just because there are people who won't let what the Bible says get in the way of what they think and do, it doesn't mean the Bible is up for a rewrite or a new interpretation. That is not negotiable. We've heard this phrase many times, "It is what it is." In this case, it's true. The Bible *is* exactly what it is—*unchangeable*!

_____

_____

_____

_____

_____

_____

_____

_____

_____

_____

_____

INTENTION IS POWERLESS

There is absolutely no power in
INTENTIONS.

Andy Andrews

I'm gonna _____ (fill in the blank). These statements are often empty words and promises. Intentions without following through turn out to be lies, but we often soften the reality by saying that we meant to do whatever, but just didn't get around to it. Then we come up with weak excuses for why we didn't do what we said we would do. This causes a huge erosion of trust. If we say we'll do something, we need to *do it*! Words are powerful, and our word is our bond—we need to honor it.

INTEGRITY

No matter how educated, talented, rich, or cool you believe you
are, how you treat people ultimately tells all.
Integrity is everything.

What is on the inside *will* come out. For Christians especially, declarations or words may be spoken, but the fruit comes from the root, and it becomes quite evident over time just how healthy the root is. Walk out the talk daily. Talk is cheap and means nothing if love, encouragement, and genuine caring is not shown to others. We don't need to be bosom buddies with everybody, but we can at least be kind and *for* them—rather than in destroy-mode *against* them.

A BETTER WORLD

I can't help thinking that this would
be a better world if everyone
would listen to God.

I think the world would be an even better place if people *did* what God said. Just listening isn't enough. Too often people hear it, and the argument begins about why their ways, thoughts and big ideas are better and higher than God's.

*** NEWSFLASH ***

Father always knows best!

_____

_____

_____

_____

_____

_____

_____

_____

_____

_____

ADVERSITY

Adversity is preparation for greatness.

Andy Andrews

The Final Summit

Too bad adversity starts so early in life before youngsters are old enough to have learned how to "fix" problems or been given permission to develop a voice to combat whatever the adversity may be. Childhood traumas and chaotic, abusive lifestyles in the home have created collateral damage by victimizing defenseless children.

Through my work experiences and even in retirement, I have worked with adults of all ages who are still reeling from hurts that were inflicted upon them when they were very young. I experience waves of sorrow when folks reveal painful pasts that still affect their current lives. The greatness that Andy refers to is a result of overcoming past wrongs, traumas, and hurts. It *can* happen. It takes time and hard work, but it is great when healing occurs. Adversity brought difficult times; overcoming adversity brings greatness.

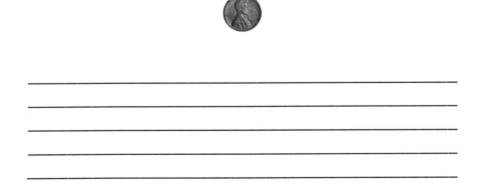

SHORT AND SIMPLE

11 Things You Need to Say Before It's Too Late

Say these things every chance you get:

I love you.

Do you need anything?

I need you.

I can do this.

You inspire me.

My life is good.

I trust you.

How can I help you?

I'm sorry.

I believe in you.

I forgive you.

Understand the value of every moment

Someday it will only be a memory

Power of Positivity

This is so good—and it doesn't require a large vocabulary. Simple statements packing so much power! This is how to let people know that you are especially fond of them.

_____
_____
_____
_____
_____
_____
_____
_____
_____
_____
_____
_____
_____
_____
_____
_____
_____
_____
_____
_____
_____
_____

**Be gentle with one another, sensitive. Forgive one another
as quickly and thoroughly as God in Christ forgave you.
Ephesians 4:32 (MSG)**

TEMPTATION

Just as roots grow stronger
when wind blows against a tree,
so every time you stand up to temptation
you become more like Jesus

Rick Warren

Purpose Driven Life

Blessed is the man who remains steadfast under trial, for when he has stood the test he will receive the crown of life, which God has promised to those who love him.
James 1:12 (ESV)

Yielding to temptation affects a Christian's ability to walk an exemplary life and weakens their testimony. What the world needs now is a major wake-up call by seeing Christians beginning to live what they say they believe. If Christians are going to live a lukewarm, wishy-washy, slipshod life using the excuse that "times have changed" to justify their actions, God's amazing grace is not being appreciated and honored at all. This is how God feels about Christians in name only:

I know you inside and out, and find little to my liking.
You're not cold, you're not hot—far better to be either cold or hot! You're stale. You're stagnant. You make me want to vomit.
Revelation 3:15 (MSG)

It's high time to *stand up strong* against every temptation Satan throws your way. Be firmly rooted in your faith, grow strong, and stand up for Jesus.

SHE BELIEVED SHE COULD, SO SHE DID

She believed she could, so she did
Because the memes told her to.
She spoke the words, but she hid
The truth, from herself and from you.

On the surface you saw her speak her belief
You saw the works of her hands
But down below was a pain she couldn't speak
And pushing it down only made it expand

So, she continued to do, to strive and labor
With immaculate selfies
Seeking people favor
And inside the content of her soul... empty

So, she wiped her tears
She smiled
20 times
To get the perfect pic
For the perfect post
In the perfect light.
Then she would swipe to filter out
Her internal light.

She read the memes but in all of her doing
In all of her branding and hustling

There was only exhaustion and zero renewing

Draining, filtered, striving, seeking, content,

"Be funny" or I'll unfollow, I'm leaving.

Strangers on screens

Living out in memes

And internally she cried out for

Peace and true meaning.

Thousands of compliments day after day

Shrinking her true purpose

That would not go away

"You're beautiful" the words became disastrous

December 31, 2018

She looked in the mirror

A broken queen

"You die tonight"

Were the words she spoke into her soul

It's time to end it all, it's time to let go

But it wasn't her body that was dying that night

It was the life she'd been living

The life that wasn't right.

As she sought sanity for the voices that ruled her

She cried out to Jesus

"Jesus, it's now or never!

If you are who you say you are

I NEED YOU NOW!"

And immediately she was in His power
His love, His grace, His healing presence
No man, no compliment, no dream had His essence
Total comfort, total connection, total everything
God's full reflection

She abandoned the meme that said
She believed she could so she did
and wrote a new one
That's no longer been hidden

She was ready to die
And in her weakness
Cried out
I SURRENDER IT ALL, LORD
Bring the pain out!
And because she believed... He did

MollyAnn Wymer Stinson

This is so relevant and restorative, full of gut-wrenching vulnerability and honesty. I spoke with Molly for the first time on December 26, 2018, and the rest is history. We have been together for some very special events, and we talk and text frequently. Molly lives 700 miles away, but she is always in my heart. She has become my "bonus daughter," and I am her "bonus mom." Her life transformation is nothing short of a miracle, and it all truly got its start with total *surrender*.

_____
_____
_____
_____
_____
_____
_____
_____
_____
_____
_____
_____
_____
_____
_____
_____
_____
_____
_____
_____
_____
_____
_____
_____

**Call upon Me in the day of trouble; I will deliver you, and
you shall glorify Me.
Psalm 50:15 (NKJV)**

WHAT REALLY MATTERS?

Your time on this earth is a gift to be used wisely.
Don't squander your words or your thoughts.
Consider that even the simplest actions
you take for your life matter beyond measure...
and they matter forever.

Andy Andrews

The author, Richard Carlson has given us the well-known books, *Don't Sweat the Small Stuff* and *It's All Small Stuff*. Due to the premise of these books, people frequently minimize situations by calling them "small stuff." However, little things combined with more little things gain momentum and become big things if they are not addressed as they pop up.

Everybody who knows me well is aware that Andy Andrews is one of my favorite authors. Regarding "small stuff," Andy's two books, *The Butterfly Effect* and *The Little Things: Why You SHOULD Sweat the Small Stuff*, helped me understand that the little things really aren't very little after all.

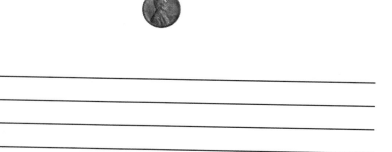

_____

_____

_____

_____

WARNING!

Give

but don't allow yourself to be used

Love

but don't allow your heart to be abused

Trust

but don't be naïve

Listen

but don't lose your voice

Great counsel! Personal responsibility is required here. It's all about setting *boundaries* and developing relationships that are safe and full of give and take. The "but" is there for a reason. It is sounding a warning, and it involves gaining perspective and learning how to achieve balance and wisdom.

_____

_____

_____

_____

_____

_____

_____

_____

_____

WHO DO YOU TRUST?

When the truth comes out, do not ask me how I knew...
ask yourself why you didn't.

There is much value in doing your own research and not being swayed by the opinions and misinformation from others. It's called integrity and wisdom.

ECHO CHAMBERS

You will never speak to anyone more than you speak to yourself in your head.
Be kind to yourself.

I t's important to learn how to speak about and to ourselves in ways that are encouraging, loving, and kind. That's the way God talks about us, so why not agree with Him? He knows what He's talking about.

I used to do an exercise with some of my groups. First, I would ask them to count to 10 out loud. Then I would ask them to cover their ears with their hands and count to 10 out loud again. I would ask, "Which is louder?" The counting always sounded louder when the ears were covered. The sound was amplified in their head. What we say to and about ourselves, even when the original messages come from others, winds up being louder and carrying more weight. Our thoughts direct our words and actions. Our actions bring about how successfully we live our lives.

Therefore, we need to be sure to echo what God says about us until it becomes our daily mantra. When that happens, our self-talk will become kind and loving rather than critical, judgmental, and lacking in acceptance. You are who God says you are, and that's the unadulterated truth. God is kind, so follow His example.

THE ARENA OF FAITH

I have often said the mind is the arena of faith;

it is where battles are won and lost.

Creflo Dollar

This is so true. Recommended reading is *The Battlefield of the Mind* by Joyce Meyer. I did a few groups using this curriculum and have kept copious notes in my Master Copies notebook. It's that good!

Here's the bottom line: Right thinking produces right living. What you think becomes your *truth*, and the quality of your life will be a direct result of how you live out your *truth*. Make sure you learn to think the way that God thinks. When you do that, the battles fought in the arena of faith are overwhelmingly won because you took the time to learn *the truth* and you've put on the full armor of God. See Ephesians 6:10-18.

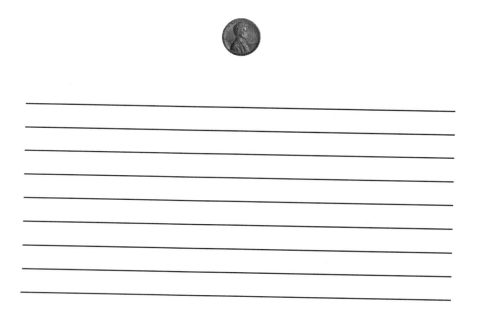

DAILY BATHS

People often say motivation doesn't last.

Well, neither does bathing,

that's why we recommend it daily.

Z i g   Z i g l a r

G reat analogy! Gotta wash the stink off! Over my lifetime, I've heard people who are in rest mode say, "My get up and go has got up and went."[1] There have been days that I've frittered away time—my do-nothing days—all the while knowing that I had plenty of things that needed attention. I learned a long time ago not to "should" on myself, but I didn't want to use that as an excuse not to be productive. At seventy-seven, my time of getting things done is becoming limited. But guess what... this morning I went straight to the shower to wash the stink off—and here I am—motivated to write.

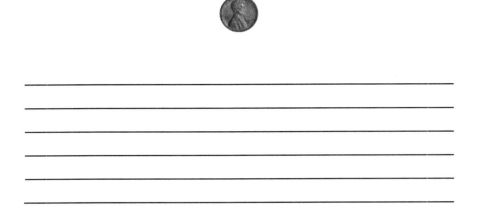

---

[1]*Chill, Grammar Police. It hurt me to write it, but that's what they said.*

LUMPY RUGS

So many things in life have been swept
under the rug. It is getting so hard to walk
upright and maintain balance.

Rowgo

This can be related to personal lives as well as things going on all around us in general. It's so easy to "sweep things under the rug" when we don't want to look at or deal with them. That practice tends to be a careless, wasteful, and negligent way to live. It lacks taking responsibility for being good stewards with the life that has been entrusted to us, and it's a glaring sign of immaturity. Avoidant behaviors are toxic and destructive and dangerous.

Sweeping things under the rug rather than dealing with them straightaway will create an unsightly pile of refuse... not unlike the local dump. As it piles up, it begins to stink. We do need to "sweat the small things" before they accumulate and become big things. We can only cover up and hide things for so long.

Perhaps it's high time to rip up our rugs and throw them out. Take a good look at the pile of refuse and have the courage and energy to clean up that neglected mess. We made it; it's our job to clean it up. We might need some help though, and that would require some humility and vulnerability on our part to reach out. But hey, that's OK and worth the risk that we may have some safe friends in our corner who are more than willing to help. We've been tripping, tiptoeing, and stumbling over this stuff with such uncertainty and fear for long enough. It's time for a fresh start with a clean slate. Sweep up the mess. Don't bother to replace the rug; it's too easy to repeat the same thing all over again. Be vulnerable enough to leave everything out in the open.

Go back to the basics. What pleases God will cause us to walk without slipping or losing our balance. Nothing hidden. Living authentically is the way to go!

MOMS

Whenever you feel discouraged, just remember, you are the center of the universe to tiny humans you made from scratch. You're kind of a big deal.

Even when moms screw up—and they will—kids long for connection with them. I have seen this happen over and over again. Kids want their mommies even when everything is in turmoil and the world seems to be upside down to them. Sometimes the moms feel like they created the chaos—maybe they did through their own choices or negligence—but the littles will still run after and hang on to their mommy for dear life. Why is that? They somehow know that mommy is *the one* who carried them to birth and beyond, and even at a very young age, they exhibit so much love and amazing grace for their mommy. People talk about the *IT* factor. Moms, in your kids' eyes, you are their *IT*, no matter what. *That* is a big deal!

Even though I have been a mom, grandma, and Oma, I still miss my mom—especially when I feel discouraged. She was always in my corner. At this point though, thanks to my mom's prayers, God is the center of my universe, but so is my mom. How can that be? I get to enjoy two-for-one, because my mom relocated to Heaven in 2005 and lives in God's presence now. *That is also a big deal!*

_____

_____

_____

FENCES

Don't worry about the grass on
the other side of the fence.
IT'S NOT YOUR GRASS!

This is a great example of how boundaries work, they have property lines. We need to tend to our own yard (life) and be good stewards or caretakers of what is ours, so it will be presentable and acceptable to everyone who happens to pass by to see how we're doing.

_____

_____

_____

_____

_____

_____

_____

_____

_____

_____

_____

_____

_____

OVERFLOW

God can't pour a one-gallon revelation into a one-cup mind.

Hugh Nibley

Interesting concept. This might encourage folks not to be so close-minded to the things that God wants to pour into them. It's kind of hard to get a full renewal of the mind if the mind of the thinker is pint-sized and unwilling to expand to receive from a big God.

**Do not conform to the pattern of this world, but be
transformed by the renewing of your mind. Then you will be
able to test and approve what God's will is—his good,
pleasing and perfect will.
Romans 12:2 (NIV)**

_____

_____

_____

_____

_____

_____

_____

_____

_____

_____

LOSSES

People always think that the most painful thing in
life is losing the one you value. The truth is, the
most painful thing is losing yourself in
the process of valuing someone too much
and forgetting that you are special too.

Simple Reminders

Oh boy... do I ever have some friends who need to see this! To develop and continue to build healthy relationships, it is crucial to become healthy and whole from the inside out. That's when there is something of real value to offer others. And, when the people picker is repaired, it is way more likely that safe people will enter the equation and stay.

_____

_____

_____

_____

_____

_____

_____

_____

_____

THE PAST BELONGS IN THE PAST

Stop replaying the past in your mind. It's gone.
Use your mental energy to manifest something new.
Don't waste your precious life force being stuck on what didn't
work out or what you could have done. Do something new today.
Each moment is another chance to recreate yourself.

The obvious message here is to keep moving forward. My friend of over sixty-five years, Mary, would say, "Onward and upward!" The word "upward" is an important one and gives me a picture of what that might look like. "Mental energy" is suggested to move into something new. I prefer to exercise "spiritual energy" as I envision moving upward. And not just any old kind of spiritual energy—the God-kind of spiritual energy is what I'm talking about.

When I think about re-creation, I don't want to be in charge of that. Recreating myself could very well turn out badly—or at least be missing some very important elements. If I trust God (I certainly do) and leave the transformation up to Him, I *know* it will turn out great.

My past has been very influential in how I turned out today, but I'm so grateful that God has shown me how to heal from past mistakes and move "onward and upward." I'm not stuck and spinning my wheels, fretting over the bonehead things I did in my past.

My prayer every day is that God will continue to work on me and help me to become the person He created me to be. A sweet song from years gone by is *Spirit of the Living God Fall Afresh on Me*, a musical request that I lift up to my loving Father often.

I'm not saying that I have this all together, that I have it
made. But I am well on my way, reaching out for Christ, who
has so wondrously reached out for me.
Philippians 3:12 (MSG)

ABUNDANCE OF THE HEART

What comes out of our hearts through the words of our mouths determines what comes to pass in our lives.

Kenneth Copeland

God knows our hearts, and He also knows that our lives reflect what we have hidden there. In Jeremiah this is painfully clear:

The heart is hopelessly dark and deceitful, a puzzle that no one can figure out. But I, God, search the heart and examine the mind. I get to the heart of the human. I get to the root of things. I treat them as they really are, not as they pretend to be.
Jeremiah 17:9-10 (MSG)

We are responsible for the words we speak—and those words are precursors of the actions that will invariably follow. If we want to enjoy our time here on earth, it behooves us to take care of our hearts and our mouths. And if we think we can get anything over on God, we need to think again. Father ALWAYS knows best, and He knows what He's talking about. Read Jeremiah 17:9-10 again for confirmation. His Word is true and will stand forever.

_____

_____

_____

_____

SOAK IT UP!

I will seek wisdom – I will listen to the counsel of wise men. The words of a wise man are like raindrops on dry ground. They are precious and can be quickly used for immediate results.

Andy Andrews

Soak up as much wisdom as you can. God knows we need it for such a time as this. Here are some words to live by:

> **Do you want to be counted wise, to build a reputation for wisdom? Here's what you do: Live well, live wisely, live humbly. It's the way you live, not the way you talk, that counts.**
> **James 3:13 (MSG)**

Andy encourages us to pay attention to the words of wise people. This verse from Proverbs confirms the benefit of doing just that:

> **Take good counsel and accept correction – that's the way to live wisely and well.**
> **Proverbs 19:20 (MSG)**

WE CAN WORK IT OUT

A little three-year-old boy was sitting on the toilet. His mother thought he had been there too long, so she went to see what was going on. The little boy was sitting on the toilet reading a book.

Every ten seconds or so, he put the book down, gripped the toilet seat with his left hand, and bopped himself on the top of his head with his right hand. His mom asked, "Billy, are you alright? You've been here quite a while."

Billy answered, "I'm fine, Mommy... I just haven't gone 'doody' yet." His mom said, "OK, you can stay here for a few more minutes... but why do you keep hitting yourself on the head?"

Billy said, "It works for ketchup."

K ids just seem to know how to work crap out. This little guy held a winning hand with a royal flush.

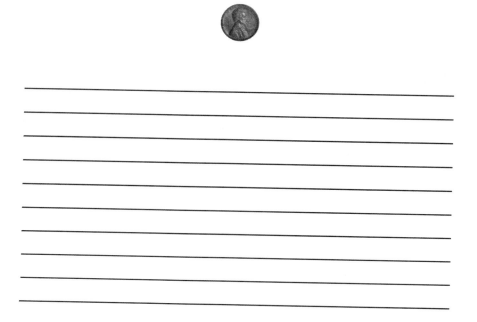

INTENTIONS: I MEANT TO...

Despite popular belief to the contrary, there is absolutely no power in intention. The seagull may intend to fly away, may decide to do so, may talk with the other seagulls about how wonderful it is to fly, but until the seagull flaps his wings and takes to the air, he is still on the dock.

There's no difference between that gull and all the others. Likewise, there is no difference in the person who intends to do things differently and the one who never thinks about it in the first place. Have you ever considered how often we judge ourselves by our intentions while we judge others by their actions? Yet intention without action is an insult to those who expected the best from you.

Andy Andrews

This is one of my favorites from *The Noticer*. Jones is talking about seagulls and people with good intentions, but he tells it like it is. Good intentions without follow-through and no intentions at all are essentially the same thing. Nothing gets done. Following thinking about it and talking about it requires real honest-to-goodness action. Flap those wings and get liftoff!

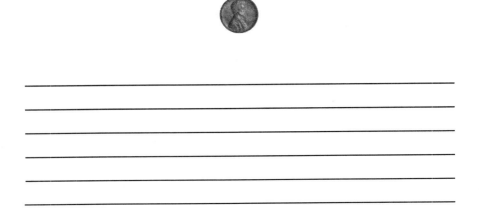

_____

_____

_____

_____

_____

THE WHO & THE DO

Our friends don't love us for what we do
Our friends love us for who we are

Many great friends love us on both counts—and take the time to voice and show their appreciation. Be sure to return the favor.

_____

_____

_____

_____

_____

_____

_____

_____

_____

_____

_____

_____

_____

_____

FIRST THINGS FIRST

Experience is the hardest kind of teacher. It gives
you the test first and the lesson afterward.

Oscar Wilde

D on't you just love pop quizzes? When you're faced with a situation that you've never encountered before, it can become a guessing game on how to proceed. Sometimes you'll guess wrong, but that's OK. At least the next time you'll know what not to do and will try something else. Lesson learned.

MOVING?

Death is just a change of address, but what you believe will determine what neighborhood you end up in.

The Christian Conservative

Location, location, location! Choose well! My change of address is in the prime location! Ultimately, everyone would like to live there, but not everyone will be accepted—there are requirements that must be met. The credit check is very specific.

_____

_____

_____

_____

_____

_____

_____

_____

_____

_____

2

FOCUSED OUTWARD

A SIGN OF MATURITY

Grace is when somebody hurts you, and you try to understand their situation instead of trying to hurt them back.

The comments to this Facebook post were interesting with one responding, "Just don't overthink it as I did for years."

I said: Good point. Even though there may be reasons that explain the hurtful actions of others toward us, there is no excuse for willfully hurting anybody. Sometimes, when overthinking a situation, we might begin to wonder how we may somehow be at fault for "causing" the hurt. That's a signal to drop it and move on. Leave the offense on the correct side of the property line.

Another said: "I call it empathy, not grace." She said grace was a gift from God and wondered if we were able to bestow grace on others. Or is God the only giver of grace?

My response: All good gifts come from God, and we extend those same gifts on to others. If we are challenged to be Christ-like, we will be "Jesus with skin" to others, exhibiting the same gifts and characteristics. Grace qualifies! Empathy is putting yourself in somebody else's shoes to understand where they're coming from. Grace is being willing to cut them some slack in the same way that God has been gracious to us even though we've been hurt. We pass it on and don't try to get even. Jesus handed us the mantle to do what He did and even greater things when He went to be with the Father. We have His Spirit hooked up with ours and are called and given the ability to be gracious, just like Him.

God's gifts are freely given with no strings attached, otherwise they wouldn't be designated "gifts." When we receive gifts, we are free to do whatever we wish to do with them. We can re-gift what God has freely given—like grace. Now it is ours to give to others. The beat goes on....

Let no corrupt word proceed out of your mouth, but what is good for necessary edification, that it may impart grace to the hearers.
Ephesians 4:29 (NKJV)

BUILDING BLOCKS

Without communication, there is no relationship.
Without respect, there is no love.
Without trust, there's no reason to continue.

Quotes Gate

There are three crucial aspects that are absolutely foundational when building connections with others. Safe people aren't 100% perfect, but they *can* be doggoned dependable in all three of the above areas. How sad it must be to read something like this and realize that current relationships have really missed hitting the bullseye. Think about it. Maybe it's time to take some affirmative action and repair or replace some connections—it's never too late.

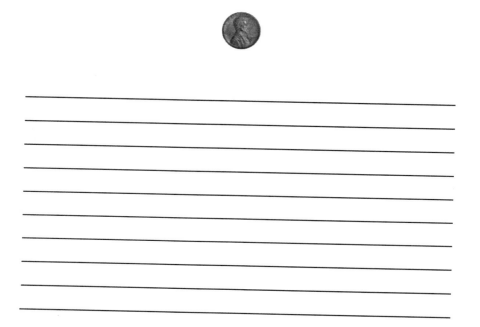

_____

_____

_____

_____

_____

_____

_____

_____

_____

_____

HUMAN CONNECTIONS: LAPTOP OR LAPTOP?

All children need a laptop. Not a computer, but a human laptop. Moms and Dads, Grammies and Grandpas, Aunts, Uncles - someone to hold them, read to them, teach them. Loved ones who will embrace them and pass on the experience, rituals, and knowledge of a hundred previous generations. Loved ones who will pass to the next generation their expectations of them, their hopes, and their dreams.

Colin Powell

We have been created for connection—and not just virtual connection to through electronic means. *Human connection!* God's plan involves relationships—real ones—with Him *and* with one another. Don't miss out on the opportunity by spending too much time on inanimate objects. Reach out and touch somebody's hand. Make this world a better place if you can.

AND THE POINT IS...

You are in a relationship to be happy, to smile, and to make good memories.
Not to be constantly upset, to feel hurt, and to cry.

WomenWorking.com

In a nutshell, this is the difference between safe people and unsafe people. There really is a way to identify the red flags and save a lot of heartache before getting too far into a toxic relationship/friendship. I have found *Safe People* by Cloud and Townsend to be an invaluable resource in learning how to identify and make safe connections.

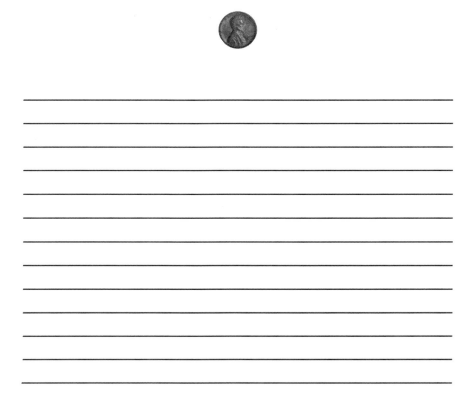

_____

_____

_____

_____

_____

_____

_____

_____

_____

_____

_____

JUDGE NOT!

Don't judge, and you won't be judged.
Don't condemn, and you won't be condemned.
Set free, and you will be set free.

Luke 6:37

On March 27, 2021, my daughter-in-law, Christy, and I talked at length about judging others and what that really looks like. What is our responsibility to others? Is correction judgment? Maybe. Some like to call it constructive criticism; others say that criticism on any level is judgment and only God can judge. Really? When we warn others—our children in particular—about actions or attitudes and possible outcomes or consequences, are we judging their choices? "If-then" warnings sound like judgments to me. Courts of law are always handing down judgments based on a preponderance or lack of evidence.

Scripture balances Scripture. The very best friends I have ever had in my rather lengthy lifetime have loved me enough to challenge me and call me out when I've messed up. Proverbs addresses this more than once. True friends will call me to a higher standard. Many might call that judgmental, but the wounds of a real friend are a gift, even when it brings discomfort and possibly a spark of anger. It can also bring Godly sorrow and repentance, thereby helping me to become who I was created to be—authentic—nothing hidden or held back.

Let's face it, the truth hurts. However, hard truth delivered lovingly, without sugar coating, may be uncomfortable to hear but brings an opportunity for healing. I would rather be corrected by friends I trust, who have my back and truly love me than be surrounded by sycophants who suck up to me with saccharine flattery. If correction is judgment, and I think it is to some extent, so be it. There will always be people who feel their toes are being stepped on and who will shout, "JUDGE NOT! Only God can judge me and tell me what to do!" These are often the same people who are unwilling to respond to correction from anyone... and certainly aren't going to let God tell them what to do. I *really* want trusted friends around me who care enough to call me out on my crap... so I can fix it. Bring it on!

By the way, this "Judge not" verse prompted me to read *all* of Luke 6. It brought more context and understanding when I read what came before and after as to why the verse was there in the first place. You might be curious about that too, so go ahead and read it.

_____

_____

_____

_____

_____

_____

_____

_____

_____

_____

_____

_____

_____

TOXIC PEOPLE

Toxic people…

Never let things go.

Can't move forward.

Bully.

Intimidate.

Lie.

Create drama.

Play the victim.

Often act out of fear and insecurity.

Take the last line of the post on toxic people and slide it to the #1 slot. That is what activates everything else. Toxic people are angry about just about everything and at everybody around them. Anger signals deeper issues, like a fear of not being able to function good enough in the world or just doing it wrong. It also signals a deep-seated lack of purpose because they don't have any idea who they are. Perhaps they have been negatively defined and affected by outside voices, or their own voice has adopted outside opinions and continues and embellishes the dialogue. If that doesn't equate to a major dose of insecurity, I don't know what does. Consequently, the anger and underlying root issues result in toxic behaviors, attitudes, and abusive language.

It isn't easy to change, but it is possible. It takes acknowledgment of the problems, a willingness to take the time to put in the hard work to turn things around, and, in all probability, a trained, skillful team to head up the program to be rid of the toxic behaviors. It's a root problem that will take some digging around to uncover the real issues that have caused toxic fruit to grow and manifest itself. Fix the root and make it healthy, and it will be possible to produce good fruit. Forget about self-help getting the job done. Self created the problem—sometimes with outside help; self needs help to fix it. Self-help all by itself rarely does the trick.

EXERCISE WISDOM

Don't mock God by continually rescuing people from their consequences.

**Do not be deceived: God cannot be mocked. A man reaps
what he sows.
Galatians 6:7**

Sometimes the best thing for a person is to reap the result of the seed they've sown. Continually bailing someone out, coddling them in their conflict, or placating their problems enables a continual cycle of mistakes because you eliminate the consequences of their error.

People don't just need relief; they need restoration. Restoration comes through taking responsibility for one's actions and changing the behaviors that produced the negative results in the first place. It doesn't just pick them up but enables them to walk.

There is only one Messiah, and it isn't us. We need to pray, "God, help me stay out of Your way by not continually rescuing people from their consequences."

Jay Jones

Continually bailing people out when they make disastrous decisions that wind up badly is enabling them to keep on doing the same thing over and over again. There is a word for that—*insanity*. Exercising wisdom when situations like this arise produces healing and restoration. Don't keep trying to be a fixer-upper by rescuing other people from their messes. It doesn't work. You'll just have to do it all over again later. Setting a boundary will put an end to rescue missions, but it will very likely provoke anger in the one who has come to expect help getting out of their messes. Stay strong though.

_____

_____

_____

_____

_____

_____

_____

_____

_____

_____

_____

_____

_____

_____

_____

_____

_____

_____

_____

_____

**A man of great wrath will suffer punishment; for if you
rescue him, you will have to do it again.
Proverbs 19:19 (NKJV)**

STAYING POWER

Time decides who you meet in your life,
your heart decides who you want in your life,
and your behavior decides who stays in your life.

WomenWorking.com

There is so much truth in all three of these elements. It pays big dividends to learn how to be a safe person and how to identify safe people to welcome into your very select circle. It is also so important to set healthy boundaries that will ensure lifelong friendships based on trust and mutual respect. That's how God's world goes around.

FOCUS

I didn't set out to be a single mom.
I set out to be the best mom I can be...
and that hasn't changed.

Not many people set out to be single parents, but it is occurring at alarming rates. Don't look to hook up in all the wrong places just to get "help" with the kids. Often, the "solution" turns out to be temporary and disruptive. It doesn't turn out well and does more harm than good. Focus on your precious kids and show them how to win at life even in the midst of adversity.

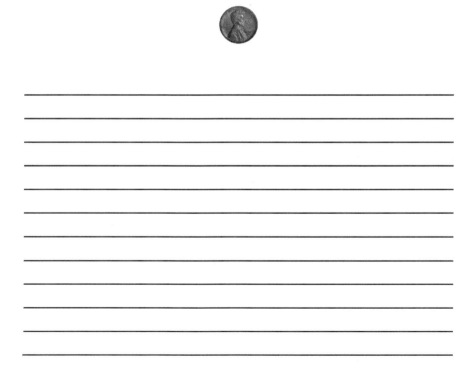

_____

_____

_____

_____

_____

_____

_____

_____

_____

_____

_____

TOO BAD, SO SAD

In a world that has become overly obsessed with feelings, I am here today to tell you this... Nobody cares how you feel. They only care how you act.

Andy Andrews

This is a tough word. It implies that you should keep your Empathy Chip in your pocket and ignore how people feel. Oh, you feel bad/angry/hurt/depressed? Too bad, so sad. That seems kind of harsh—even un*feel*ing—if I can say that. But I think I understand what Andy is saying here.

Feelings are so doggoned fickle and all over the place. We need to get a grip. Actions speak volumes. If feelings govern our lives, we will lack stability. However, if we can override our emotions and learn how to function well and exhibit some strong, positive character traits, we will gain greater favor and acceptance from others. Put the emotive drama and "pity party" behaviors aside and live a life of integrity that matters.

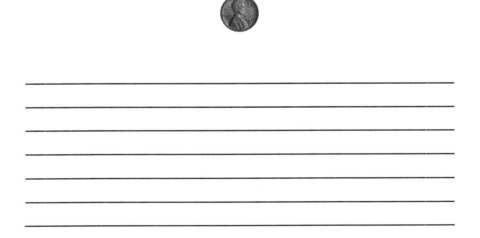

TRUTH BE TOLD

Those who can manage to make truth a part of their character will rise to the top. Their character will be recognized, and people will follow... they will follow the truth.

Andy Andrews

To say that telling the truth is one of the top character traits that I value in my family and with my friends would be an enormous understatement. Those are my very special safe people, and it's easy for me to trust them with my life.

_____

_____

_____

_____

_____

_____

_____

_____

_____

_____

_____

_____

HEALTHY BOUNDARIES

Are your boundaries healthy?

Whatever you allow to happen will keep on happening.

Lynda Field

The operative words are "you allow." When people are saying and doing things that feel like an invasion of your life and space, realize that you must exercise personal responsibility to protect what is yours—your peace, joy, and quality of life. The enemy comes to steal, kill, and destroy (John 10:10a) and way too often, people are the messengers who come to trespass your borders. There is one word that can be used to turn back this onslaught, *NO!* Nothing will ever change if nothing is ever done. Develop healthy boundaries!

ACT YOUR AGE

I don't know how to act my age.
I've never been this age before.

If I had used my paternal grandparents as role models, my life would be very different today. They didn't look or act like me at all. They rarely left their designated easy chairs and didn't appear to enjoy life very much. They were old stick-in-the-muds who hardly ever smiled. Their expressions were so dour. I can't remember ever hearing them laugh. Very sad. Here's the thing though, my paternal grandparents were the same age at that time that I am now. I don't look like they looked, and I certainly am not acting like them either. I'm not entirely sure how I'm supposed to act, but I'm glad "my age" doesn't look like what it used to look like. They don't look the same by a long shot.

My dad, having grown up in that atmosphere, tended to be more reserved, stoic, and stern. Thankfully, my mom's family was quite the opposite. Their home was full of laughter and good times. In an already large family, they always welcomed "just one more" to the table. My mom brought that same spirit into my childhood home. She created an atmosphere of love, generosity, laughter, and fun shenanigans in our home. I'm so thankful for that. These days, "old" doesn't look at all like it was in the olden days. I think I'm rocking it and definitely NOT acting my age by the old standards. Times have changed!

_____
_____
_____
_____
_____
_____
_____
_____
_____
_____
_____
_____
_____
_____
_____
_____
_____
_____
_____
_____
_____
_____
_____

(The righteous) will still bear fruit in old age; they will stay
fresh and green
Psalm 92:14 (NIV)

I HAVE A RULE

Several years ago, I was accosted by a drunk neighbor who did not like the way I had parked my car on the street. It became clear about a minute into the conversation that he was not going to be reasonable. I just interrupted and said, "I am sorry, but I have a rule. I don't talk to people who are intoxicated. Call me tomorrow and I will be glad to discuss this." And I walked off, with him screaming all the way. I never heard from him, as he probably did not even remember the incident, but what stood out to me was what happened with the friend who was with me.

She told me that that little rule changed her entire relationship with a difficult person in her life. She had never thought about it, but she could have rules that she lived by, and not talking to someone screaming at her could be one of those. It's a small thing, but for her it was a big one.

There may be people in your life with whom you are getting negative results, and with whom you need some rules. And remember, these are not rules for them, but for you. In the conversation with the drunk, notice that I did not say he was not allowed to talk to me that way. He could do whatever he wanted.

Instead, I said that I did not allow myself to talk to someone who was TWI (talking while intoxicated). That is a big difference. The rule is for you, not the other person. Let him talk all he wants. I just won't be there listening.

Dr. Henry Cloud

The One-Life Solution

Brilliant! This is a great lesson for anyone who would like to shun negative drama in their life. You can't *make* anyone do anything with any success if they don't want to do it, but you *can* decide what you will tolerate and/or allow—and to what extent you will participate in such foolish nonsense. You decide. Make your own rules and follow them. Develop your own Game of Life by writing clear and concise rules for how you are willing to participate in your game with others—and don't cheat. Cheaters never win!

_____

_____

_____

_____

_____

_____

_____

_____

_____

_____

_____

_____

_____

_____

_____

_____

_____

_____

_____

And whoever will not receive you nor hear your words, when you depart from that house or city, shake off the dust from your feet.
Matthew 10:14 (NKJV)

WHY ARE YOU SORRY?

Here's the thing about sorry; it's just a word. It doesn't erase what you did, it doesn't fix anything. It's an acknowledgment. It's everything you do after the sorry that proves if you really are.

Stephanie Bennett-Henry

Apologies often are offered quickly, without much thought, just to get people off our back so we can move on past whatever happened. Not much thought is given to it, and it means next to nothing. Even parents will tell their kids to say, "Sorry" to just about everything, so they do. Are they sorry they were caught—or sorry for what they did? We need to ask ourselves the same questions. To top off the perfunctory "Sorry," the equally quick "I forgive you" is the expected response. That little exchange is way too easy and doesn't solve a thing.

Here's an idea: Whenever we hear the word "sorry," let's ask some questions. What are you sorry about? What did you do? How do you think what you did or said affected me? Don't accept a blanket "sorry" without talking about it. This is an opportunity to connect for real. Perhaps the offender might even learn how to gain some insight and develop an empathy chip. When we cross the line and mess up, we often know exactly what we're doing, and we also know it's the wrong thing to do. If someone is truly sorry, the apology will also bring about changed behaviors.

_____
_____
_____
_____
_____
_____
_____
_____
_____
_____
_____
_____
_____
_____
_____
_____
_____
_____
_____
_____
_____

**Be kind to one another, tenderhearted, forgiving one
another, as God in Christ forgave you.
Ephesians 4:32 (NKJV)**

THE SECRET OF SUCCESS

"Sir, what is the secret of your success?" a reporter asked a bank president.

"Two words."

"And, sir, what are they?"

"Good decisions."

"And how do you make good decisions?"

"One word."

"And, sir, what is that?"

"Experience."

"And how do you get experience?"

"Two words."

"And, sir, what are they?"

"Bad decisions."

Joyce Meyer citing an anonymous source

Making Good Habits, Breaking Bad Habits

I really liked the simplicity of this exchange. Now the key is rising to the challenge of *learning* from the bad decisions that have caused trainwrecks in our lives. The learning part and not repeating bad decisions will bring about the successes in life that we all would like to enjoy.

ENTER THE RING

Relationships are worth fighting for,

but you can't be the only one fighting.

I know so many people who have felt this way. When the fight is one-sided, it isn't a fair fight. Some relationships were *not* developed well in the first place, so toxic, hurtful fights were inevitable—and *not* for the purpose of working toward harmony. On the other hand, if a relationship is deemed to be salvageable, work together with everything you've got to make it work. A restored relationship is worth the effort.

_____

_____

_____

_____

_____

_____

_____

_____

_____

_____

_____

_____

PICK-ME-UPS

Friends pick us up when we fall down, and if they can't pick us up, they lie down and listen for a while.

This is the very best kind of friend to have—safe and worth their weight in gold. This is an extremely rare commodity these days. I have a few—do you?

_____

_____

_____

_____

_____

_____

_____

_____

_____

_____

_____

_____

_____

_____

THE MOUTH/EAR CONNECTIONS

What should not be heard by little ears,

should not be said by big mouths.

Come on, people—speak blessings, not cursings. Be great role models for those precious children you are training for life. Don't put yourself in the position of having to correct inappropriate language and behaviors later due to the examples you set for them in their early years. Take yourself to the woodshed and straighten up and fly right, so you won't have to deal with a "mini you" later.

_____

_____

_____

_____

_____

_____

_____

_____

_____

_____

_____

DO YOU HAVE ANY FRIENDS?

Everybody is not your friend. Just because they hang around you and laugh with you doesn't mean they are your friend. People pretend well. At the end of the day, real situations expose fake people... so pay attention.

O ver time, the true character of a person, good or bad, will rise to the surface and mix in with the outward behaviors and attitudes. Pay close attention to the signals. Stick with the safe people who do the following three things:

1) Bring you closer to God.

2) Encourage you to have more safe friends, not just them.

3) Help you become your best self—the one you were created to be.

_____

_____

_____

_____

_____

_____

_____

_____

_____

_____

NO-MATTER-WHAT FRIENDS

Respect people who find time for you in their busy schedule,
but love people who never look at their schedule when you need them.

It's rare, but there really are the "no-matter-what" friends. You will always find them in your corner. It might take a while to find them, but, when you do, they will never leave you in the lurch. They will be there for the long haul.

GRANDPA'S FACE

A little girl was sitting next to her grandfather as he read her a bedtime story.

From time to time, she would take her eyes off the book and reach up and touch his wrinkled cheek. She touched her own cheek after she touched his.

After a little while of thinking, she asked, "Grandpa, did God make you?"

He looked at her and said, "Yes, sweetheart, God made me a long time ago."

She paused for a few seconds and then asked, "Grandpa, did God make me too?"

He replied, "Yes, pumpkin, God made you just a little while ago."

Feeling their respective faces again, she whispered to him,

"God's getting better at it, isn't He?"

S ome things I have included in this book are stand-alone pieces that don't require my two cents. This is one example.

_____

_____

_____

_____

_____

_____

_____

_____

_____

A GOOD RELATIONSHIP WITH A BAD PERSON?

Contrary to Christian teaching, not every bad relationship can be restored. Sadly, that false hope has kept some very good people "chained" to some very bad people. The good person stays and prays, believes, forgives, compromises, tries, tries again, yields, forgives, suffers, and forgives again---sometimes for years. But nothing changes. Nothing is repaired. Nothing is restored!

The truth of the matter is that one cannot have a good relationship with a bad person. The problem, in fact, is not really a relationship problem; the problem is the people in the relationship.

The painful truth is that no amount of prayer, love, faith, time, or effort can change a person who does not want to change. And, truth be told, as long as the bad person is accommodated and enabled by the good person, there is no compelling reason for the bad person to change. This is a hard truth, but is the truth nonetheless.

There comes a time in a bad relationship for the good person to cut the chain and un-bind themselves from the bad person. Although the good person will most often feel guilty and feel selfish and feel unloving, when they do this, their action is often not unloving or selfish, but is an act of wisdom. By taking this action, they not only depart from a situation where they will likely become unwell themselves and a situation which renders them unable to truly care for others; they also remove the disincentive for the bad person to change. Enabling bad behavior is not charitable, kind, or godly.

Nothing can steal your joy, tap your strength, paralyze you, and render you useless like a profound relationship with a bad person. Do NOT enter into one! And if you are in one, pray for wisdom and strength and direction, realizing that a good relationship with a bad person is not possible!

Sometimes—not always—but sometimes, you will have to unchain yourself in order to remain or become healthy.

Guy Duininck

I am 1000% on board with this very powerful, strong, and important word from Guy. Sometimes, when the fight and effort to make personal changes to strengthen and enhance a troubled relationship doesn't get met with reciprocal efforts by the other person, it becomes quite clear that it is a losing battle. Letting go is hard to do, especially when the desire was for reconciliation. However, going back and settling for the same ol' same ol' is counterproductive and ultimately ends with regret and failure. Ya gotta know when to hold 'em, know when to fold 'em, know when to walk away, and know when to run.

When boundaries are violated, disrespect is rampant, and abuses are unfettered, RUN! Nobody has the right or the ability to change anyone other than themselves. If the other person is unwilling to see a need to change and is unwilling to surrender, nobody can make it happen—not even God. He won't violate anybody's will by forcing the issue, but He may remove His favor and blessing.

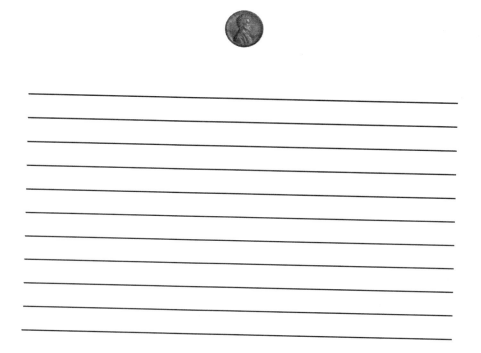

HIGHER STANDARDS

Most folks figure a true friend is someone who accepts them as they are, but that's dangerous garbage to believe. A true friend holds you to a higher standard. A true friend brings out the best in you.

Andy Andrews

According to Proverbs 17:17, friends love through all kinds of weather. A real friend will love at all times, but that's not the same thing as acceptance. I believe that Proverbs 27:6, which talks about the wounds of a friend being faithful, refers to tough confrontational situations. We love our friends too much to leave them where they are when their behaviors and attitudes leave much to be desired.

I want my friends to call me out when I'm messing up and need to grow up in areas. None of us have arrived yet, and a great friend will be honest enough with us let us know when we must step it up a notch.

Friends love through all kinds of weather, and families stick together in all kinds of trouble.
Proverbs 17:17 (MSG)

_____

_____

_____

_____

_____

LIFE-O-SUCTION

What happens while listening to people who drain us of all energy as they talk about their endless drama and escapades.

Rowgo

This is a play on the word "liposuction" that involves suction to reduce bulk. As a therapist there were times I felt sucked dry by endless accounts of life events that often sounded like pity parties and blame games. Personal responsibility was a rarity. One day the word "life-o-suction" popped into my head. That was it! Finally, a word—my word—to explain what it feels like when this happens.

I ran across something Lysa Terkeurst said that just about wraps up how words can impact others: "We can use our words to breathe life into another person or we can use our words to suck the life right out of them. Our choice."

FRONT BURNER

Children are not a distraction from more important work.
They are the most important work.

C.S. Lewis

Before bringing children into this world, we need to thoughtfully and prayerfully consider how their presence will impact our lives. Some people say, "My children are my life." They certainly do need to be a very large part of it, because they are depending on us to let them know how important and loved they are. It is our responsibility, as parents, to keep our children on the front burner, so we can always keep a close eye on them. Children who are relegated to back burners often get burned due to neglect.

SOUL FOOD

*There are SO many times when we need our children more than they need us!
They have no idea what they truly do for our soul!*

Later in life, this becomes more and more prevalent and true. Time spent with my kids is priceless! Even though they live busy lives and have many responsibilities, I cherish the times we can come together and talk about things that matter. Getting help with chores and technology is becoming more of a thing for me, but being a huge people person, I *love* getting together and just talking.

For several years, I have visited Russ and his family on Saturdays. I have even been able to help out with some various jobs that needed to be done, but truth be told, it has been more difficult to lend much of a hand with physical activities. This body of mine has been around for close to eighty years, and it isn't nearly as strong and flexible as it used to be. However, my mouth works just fine—*and everybody said "Amen."* So, conversation is still my forte. Talking about things that matter every week fills up my love tank to overflowing.

When Mara gets a break in her very busy schedule, we get together and share love, laughter, and tears as we enjoy heartfelt conversations. And, when I say that Mara "has my back," she knows exactly what that means. It may even produce a chuckle.

My kids are my soul food, and they always fill me up. So thankful!

_____

_____

_____

_____

_____

_____

_____

_____

_____

_____

_____

_____

_____

_____

_____

_____

_____

_____

_____

_____

_____

_____

_____

_____

**Train up a child in the way he should go, and when he is old
he will not depart from it.
Proverbs 22:6 (NKJV)**

TRANSFORMERS UNITE!

Sometimes people try to expose what's wrong with you because they can't handle what's right about you.

I can think of a few people who deal with this on a regular basis. Often the critics haven't dealt with or even recognized their own issues, so they tend to shoot down the efforts and successes of those who are beginning to take responsibility for their own lives. The critics tend to accentuate the negative in others and try to minimize or eliminate their positive characteristics. Transformers, on the other hand, are leaving their pasts behind and moving toward their cheerleaders and coaches for healthy encouragement. They need to distance themselves from the naysayers and dream bashers.

_____

_____

_____

_____

_____

_____

_____

_____

_____

_____

PLEASANT DREAMS

Fill your children with good thoughts before they go to bed. Ask them about their favorite part of the day, praise them for a good deed, pray with them, and tell them they're the best gift God ever gave you. They'll fall asleep feeling ten feet tall.

David Young

A Little Guide to a Big Life

PSA to my grands (Stephen, Christina, Samantha) and all parents of young children:

As kids grow older, they will remember and cherish the intimate, loving attention given to them.

There are times when bedtime for the littles finally arrives after a very long, challenging, and tiring day, and the parents, who are longing for a little peace and quiet and "me" time, are beyond ready to scoot them off to bed quickly without another word. Put your "needs" on hold for a few more minutes and grab the opportunity to cap off your kids' day in the most positive way possible. Bedtime *can* be a very special—even sacred—time.

For too many kids, bedtime is quite the opposite. It can be a scary time, lacking a sense of safety and protection. What they hear is a frustrated and angry "GO TO BED—NOW!" Perhaps they *were* a handful every minute of the day. You're the grownup though and their world revolves around *you*. They *depend* on you, they *need* you and they need to *know* that you still love them—*no matter what*. Besides, you are responsible for them being here in the first place.

Muster up a bit more time, energy, and patience to finish off their day with a little intimate, quiet, and peaceful connection filled with love and appreciation for those precious lives that have been entrusted to your care. Your kids *will* remember and thank you later. Give them the biggest gift of all—great memories.

_____
_____
_____
_____
_____
_____
_____
_____
_____
_____
_____
_____
_____
_____
_____
_____
_____
_____
_____

TRUST MUSCLES

Never trust someone that has let you down more than two times.
Once was a *warning*, twice was a *lesson*, and anything more than that is simply just taking advantage.

The word "Never" may seem strong and harsh, but any kind of a betrayal damages the trust muscle. It takes a long time and a consistent, sustained change of behavior as well as much conversation before daring to trust again. Empty words and "sorry" without noticeable changes just aren't good enough.

_____

_____

_____

_____

_____

_____

_____

_____

_____

_____

PEOPLE-PLEASERS

Quit trying to please everyone. Get this through your head... you are not responsible for other people's happiness. It is exclusively other people's responsibility to please themselves. Be authentic and please yourself, which is perfect for running off the people who need to go and bringing in the people who should be in your life.

We sure aren't taught this as children, are we? When children are taught to be "good" and keep everyone happy, it teaches them that they have the impossible burden of being responsible for other people's happiness. It teaches them that other people's happiness comes before theirs, and they wrap that concept up in a suffocating package called "not being selfish." And what do you get for this so-called "not being selfish"? Acceptance... but sadly, a false acceptance for being someone you are not. I didn't say it, but we have surely all heard it, "to thine own self be true."

Get selfish and quit worrying about other people's happiness. You are responsible for your happiness. Take care of yourself. If you try to make everyone happy, everyone will be happy but you. You will never make people happier than by being a happy person yourself.

Bryant McGill

I'm not an advocate of selfish behavior, but *self-care* is important. There is a difference. And we are called to exercise self-control. This is an enormous boundary issue, and wrong teachings and mindsets have muddied the waters. Our job is to take responsibility *for ourselves* and to be responsible *to others* in ways that do not infringe upon their freedom to make their own choices without our interference. It is NOT our job to "make" other people happy.

_____
_____
_____
_____
_____
_____
_____
_____
_____
_____
_____
_____
_____
_____
_____
_____
_____
_____
_____
_____
_____

**Am I now trying to win the approval of human beings, or of
God? Or am I trying to please people? If I were still trying to
please people, I would not be a servant of Christ.
Galatians 1:10 (NIV)**

BUILDING STEPS

Letting go of toxic people is a step towards being happier.

It's also a step toward making healthier choices and becoming wiser in building safe relationships. When that happens, *joy* begins to join in with happiness. As toxic people are removed, there is more room for genuine friendships that will last and bring great fulfillment and purpose for living.

_____

_____

_____

_____

_____

_____

_____

_____

_____

_____

_____

_____

_____

_____

MAKE YOUR OWN CHANGE

Allow your partner to fully be themselves, then determine if they are good for you. Rather than setting rules and making them change, so that they are good for you by default.

Mark Sutton

This works so much better for friendships too. The key is knowing them long enough for the real person to emerge. They may try to change or appear to change for you if they believe it will win you over or gain an advantage but be careful here. That kind of "change" doesn't last very long due to insincere motivations. Trying to keep up with the facade is exhausting.

And remember, nobody has the power or the right to change another person—it's a boundary issue. True change doesn't occur from external pressure or nagging. It's an inside out thing when insight is gained. That's when a person realizes that changing would be personally beneficial. Everybody needs to own their own need for change—and then *do it*. This will keep all of us busy enough working on our own stuff and will leave us zero time to butt into anybody else's business or push for their need to change.

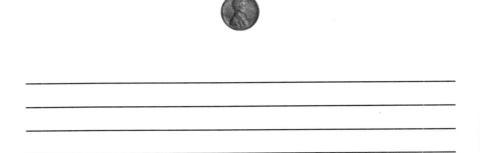

GREED OR GOOD STEWARDSHIP

I have never understood why it is 'greed'
to want to keep the money you have earned,
but not greed to take somebody else's money.

Thomas Sowell

Please, can someone help me understand that concept? Do I not have the right to keep and govern that which is mine? Jesus tells a parable in Matthew 20:1-16 to illustrate ownership and boundaries. Read it—*please!*

I am not wealthy, but I have been blessed with enough. Because I have been a good steward with what God has entrusted to me, people who know me well are aware that my desire is to be generous with my various resources—time, skills, and money. I love being able to do that, *but* it is *my* choice to do so.

_____
_____
_____
_____
_____
_____
_____
_____

TO LOVE & TO HATE ARE CHOICES

People are going to love you or hate you.

Don't waste time trying to control that.

Spend your days pleasing God, not people.

I want to hear God say, "Well done, my good and faithful servant."

There are also people who will barely tolerate you or will appear to be a friend, while being critical and judgmental of you behind your back. You can't be a people-pleaser and expect everything to be A-OK. Be a God-pleaser. God's plan has always involved building relationships with others too. He doesn't want people to live in isolation to avoid being hurt by others, but there are enough safe people in the world who are "Jesus with skin on" who can fill up your love tank. That's more than enough!

DON'T BE AN ENABLER

Don't handicap your children by making their lives easy.

Robert Heinlein

God enables us to do the right thing which, believe it or not, is to encourage our children to take on the responsibility of doing what they have been taught and required to do for themselves. That's how they learn and mature. Don't be a harmful enabler.

SUCCESSFUL TRANSITION

A mother's job is to teach her children to not need her anymore.
The hardest part of that job is accepting success.

It's funny how that works. As I grew into adulthood and became more independent, I didn't *need* my mom as much, but I *wanted* her in my life more and more. I would call that transition a success!

_____

_____

_____

_____

_____

_____

_____

_____

_____

_____

_____

_____

_____

_____

WELCOME TO LIFE

People will let you down -

welcome to life.

People will also lift you up, save you,

love you, embrace you, teach

you, and guide you.

Welcome to life!

Elle Febbo

Nobody is 100% safe, but there are some awesome safe people around. Learn what to look for while you are learning how to develop your own safe traits. Develop and grow so you can enjoy a life worth living. It's an adventure!

_____

_____

_____

_____

_____

_____

_____

_____

IT'S NOT ALL ABOUT YOU

I thought about quitting,

but then I noticed who was watching.

If you're a parent, it's not all about you anymore. You brought your children into the world, and quitting is not a fair option—although there are parents who do just that. Abandoning your children when the going gets tough is so unfair, unloving, and a very selfish thing to do. Get your issues together and get help if needed. Your children will always be able to sense when danger is present. Alleviate their fears and step up and do whatever is required to fix things. It was your choice to become a parent, so *be one* and *don't quit!*

_____

_____

_____

_____

_____

_____

_____

_____

_____

_____

THE BLACK TELEPHONE

When I was a young boy, my father had one of the first telephones in our neighborhood. I remember the polished, old case fastened to the wall. The shiny receiver hung on the side of the box. I was too little to reach the telephone, but I used to listen with fascination when my mother talked to it.

Then I discovered that somewhere inside the wonderful device lived an amazing person. Her name was "Information Please," and there was nothing she did not know. Information Please could supply anyone's number and the correct time.

My personal experience with the genie-in-a-bottle came one day while my mother was visiting a neighbor. Amusing myself at the tool bench in the basement, I whacked my finger with a hammer. The pain was terrible, but there seemed no point in crying because there was no one home to give sympathy. I walked around the house sucking my throbbing finger, finally arriving at the stairway.

The telephone! Quickly, I ran for the footstool in the parlor and dragged it to the landing. Climbing up, I unhooked the receiver in the parlor and held it to my ear. "Information please," I said into the mouthpiece just above my head.

A click or two and a small clear voice spoke into my ear.

"Information."

"I hurt my finger...," I wailed into the phone. The tears came readily now that I had an audience.

"Isn't your mother home?" came the question.

"Nobody's home but me," I blubbered.

"Are you bleeding?" the voice asked.

"No," I replied. "I hit my finger with the hammer and it hurts."

"Can you open the icebox?" she asked.

I said I could.

"Then chip off a little bit of ice and hold it to your finger," said the voice.

After that, I called "Information Please" for everything. I asked her for help with my geography, and she told me where Philadelphia was. She helped me with my math. She told me my pet chipmunk, that I had caught in the park just the day before, would eat fruit and nuts.

Then there was the time Petey, our pet canary, died. I called "Information Please" and told her the sad story. She listened, and then said things grown-ups say to soothe a child. But I was not consoled.

I asked her, "Why is it that birds should sing so beautifully and bring joy to all families, only to end up as a heap of feathers on the bottom of a cage?"

She must have sensed my deep concern, for she said quietly, "Wayne, always remember that there are other worlds to sing in." Somehow, I felt better.

Another day I was on the telephone, "Information Please."

"Information," said the now familiar voice.

"How do I spell fix?" I asked.

All this took place in a small town in the Pacific Northwest. When I was nine years old, we moved across the country to Boston. I missed my friend very much.

"Information Please" belonged in that old wooden box back home, and I somehow never thought of trying the shiny new phone that sat on the table in the hall. As I grew into my teens, the memories of those childhood conversations never really left me. Often, in moments of doubt and perplexity, I would recall the serene sense of security I had then. I appreciated now how patient, understanding, and kind she was to have spent her time on a little boy.

A few years later, on my way west to college, my plane put down in Seattle. I had about a half-hour or so between planes. I spent 15 minutes or so on the phone with my sister, who lived there now. Then, without thinking what I was doing, I dialed my hometown operator and said, "Information Please."

Miraculously, I heard the small, clear voice I knew so well. "Information."

I hadn't planned this, but I heard myself saying, "Could you please tell me how to spell fix?"

There was a long pause. Then came the soft-spoken answer, "I guess your finger must have healed by now."

I laughed. "So, it's really you," I said. "I wonder if you have any idea how much you meant to me during that time.

"I wonder," she said, "if you know how much your calls meant to me. I never had any children, and I used to look forward to your calls."

I told her how often I had thought of her over the years, and I asked if I could call her again when I came back to visit my sister.

"Please do," she said. "Just ask for Sally."

Three months later I was back in Seattle. A different voice answered, "Information." I asked for Sally.

"Are you a friend?" she asked.

"Yes, a very old friend," I answered.

"I'm sorry to tell you this," she said. "Sally had been working part-time the last few years because she was sick. She died five weeks ago."

Before I could hang up, she said, "Wait a minute. Is your name Wayne?"

"Yes," I answered.

"Well, Sally left a message for you She wrote it down in case you called. Let me read it to you."

The note said, "Tell Wayne there are other worlds to sing in. He'll know what I mean."

I thanked her and hung up. I knew what Sally meant.

Never underestimate the impression you may make on others. Whose life have you touched today?

I'm wondering how many people can relate to a story like this one. Connecting with people quite by accident can add so much flavor, significance, and sustenance to a life. I like to call these delightful connections *Godwinks*. It's as if God sees us in whatever situation we're in and seizes the opportunity to surprise us with something out of the blue and totally unexpected. Because He loves us so much and wants to bless us, He gives us a little wink and says, "I see you. Here, this is just for you!" Very often, He uses people to deliver His *Godwinks*. Be a noticer and keep an eye out for them. You'll know them when you see them.

_____
_____
_____
_____
_____
_____
_____
_____
_____
_____
_____
_____
_____
_____
_____
_____
_____
_____
_____

Perfume and incense bring joy to the heart, and the pleasantness of a friend springs from their heartfelt advice.
Proverbs 27:9 (NIV)

REFRESHING

Love isn't what you say.

Love is what you do.

Often there's a big difference between these two things. How refreshing it is when they look and sound the same. Let your words line up with your actions. Say what you mean and mean what you say, and make sure to follow through with the actions that match your heartfelt intentions.

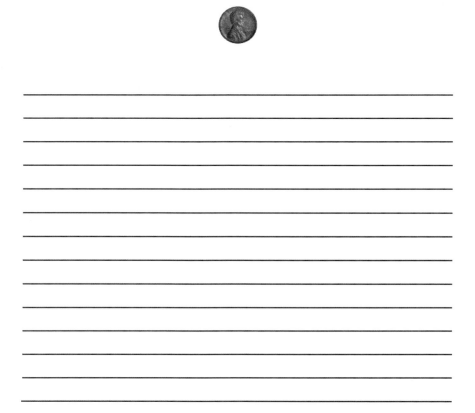

_____

_____

_____

_____

_____

_____

_____

_____

_____

_____

_____

_____

CONTROLLERS

Controllers Come In Two Types

Aggressive Controllers – These people clearly don't listen to others' boundaries. They run over other people's fences like a tank. They are sometimes verbally abusive, sometimes physically abusive. But most of the time, they simply aren't aware that others even have boundaries.

It's as if they live in a world of "Yes." There is no place for someone else's "No." They attempt to get others to change, to make the world fit their idea of the way life should be. They neglect to accept their own responsibility to accept others as they are.

Manipulative Controllers – Less honest than the aggressive controller, manipulators try to persuade others out of their boundaries. They talk others into "Yes." They indirectly manipulate circumstances to get their way, they seduce others into carrying their burdens, they use guilt messages. Manipulators deny their desire to control others; they brush aside their own self-centeredness.

Dr. Henry Cloud & Dr. John Townsend

One type is outrageous; the other is sneaky but becomes very predictable over time. The aggressive controllers are abusive; the manipulators are passive-aggressive with abusive tendencies too. In both cases, boundaries that have been set by the people in the controllers' lives are totally disregarded. Does that mean that people with boundaries should abandon the fences they have learned how to put up and allow themselves to be run over by controllers? The answer to that ridiculous question is a big, fat NO! They got the message from somewhere that boundaries are a good thing to have for their own safety and freedom. They need to send their own message of how much they are willing to endure before they walk away.

Nobody has the right to control the lives of others, and anybody who allows that to happen is giving their life and their freedom away to people who have no right to it. Don't allow that to happen. Take back control of your own life!

_____

_____

_____

_____

_____

_____

_____

_____

_____

_____

_____

_____

_____

_____

_____

_____

_____

_____

_____

EYE CANDY

The same people who are candy to our eyes can be poison to our hearts.
Study their ingredients before feeding them to your soul.

L earn how to identify the people who will fill you up with good things that are safe and nutritious for your soul. While shopping for groceries, we will often carefully check the ingredients of food items to make sure we won't be ingesting anything harmful. We need to be as cautious when we select our friends, so that our hunger for healthy, safe relationships is fully satisfied. One final note: be sure to check the expiration date.

DEFINE "LONELY"

People think being alone makes you lonely, but I don't think that's true. Being surrounded by the wrong people is the loneliest thing in the world.

Kim Culbertson

Living a life well will have purpose and significance. God's plan makes a big difference in the quality of life we lead. It wasn't designed to be lived in a vacuum and isolated from others. We were created for relationship—with God and with people. Connecting with safe, caring people matters, because that is how we internalize the good stuff that fills up our love tank. Then we are also able to spend time alone because we are not trying to run on fumes. Being surrounded by safe people who value and support us will never leave us feeling lonely. Choose well.

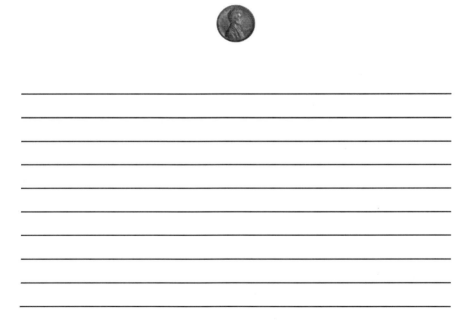

HIGH OCTANE

People are the fuel for us to go, be healthy, and prosper. God created a system in which we are to need not only Him, but also one another. We need to know what we need, recognize who can supply it, and have the skills to get it.

Dr. John Townsend
People Fuel

Reflecting back over seven-plus decades, I'm able to identify the people in my life who have absolutely added high-octane fuel to my life. They have helped me to grow and go. These special connections over the years have helped me to develop and become who I was created to be. If you are reading this and are remembering good times, you know who you are. Accept my heartfelt love and thanks.

SYCOPHANTS

Most people don't really want the truth. They just
want constant reassurance that what
they believe is the truth.

A sycophant is a person who acts obsequiously toward someone important to gain advantage. Obsequious people are usually not being genuine in their eagerness to serve. They resort to flattery to stay in the good graces of authority figures—teachers, pastors, bosses, politicians, parents, and more. Sycophants are always "yes people" and often referred to as brownnosers, bootlickers, or toadies. There are plenty of them around, and they are constantly fawning over and reassuring the people who crave undying allegiance, even though their "truths" and beliefs may be skewed and lacking accuracy and credibility.

FAMILY DNA

You don't tolerate something just because you have DNA in common.

As much as we would love to believe and long for acceptable and loving behaviors within our own family circles, that doesn't happen as often as we would like. My dad would always say "Peace at any price", but once I was older, I realized that was a statement without boundaries. That was a somewhat flawed way of saying just drop whatever was going on, don't belabor the issue, and go on as if nothing is wrong. That type of "solution" never solved a thing. The problem behaviors and attitudes needed to be confronted and handled, so that real peace could be restored in the home. Some families have figured this out and work hard at restoration; other families continue to behave badly.

Regarding setting boundaries in the home, try stating this:

"NO! That behavior (or attitude or language or whatever) is NOT acceptable, and it needs to stop right now. You're a member of this family, and I love you too much to allow you to continue talking or behaving that way!"

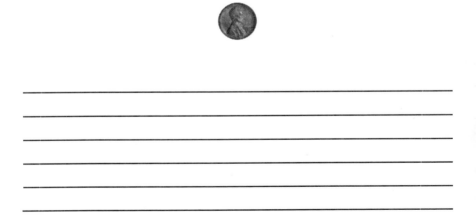

VULNERABILITY

It's time to be vulnerable with someone this week.

Vulnerability, or the act of expressing a need or weakness to another person, is one of the greatest keys to happiness and a fulfilled life. You may need to be vulnerable with someone about a loss or failure in your life. Or it could be about a struggle that not many people know about. Or it could simply be a need to vent about a burden, just so that someone can help bear it with you.

Vulnerability has three benefits for you.

1) that you know you are not alone.

2) that you are known and no longer unknown.

3) that you are strengthened to face challenges and push on.

That is how important vulnerability is.

At the same time, it can be scary. What if the person thinks less of you, judges you, or is not responsive? What if they distance from you? These are all real risks, so choose carefully who you are vulnerable with. I would rather have just a few friends with whom I am totally transparent, than a great many acquaintances who don't really know my insides. Take the risk.

Dr. John Townsend

It's easy to be around a lot of people, but it's not prudent to share your heart and concerns haphazardly. Becoming vulnerable with your business for all to see, especially publicly on social media sites, is especially foolish. Not everyone will react to your troubles or opinions in a supportive fashion. There is too much hatred and anger going around these days. Don't spill your guts to total strangers or people you don't know well who have no problem bashing, bullying, and ripping you apart when you become vulnerable in the wrong arena. Use discretion, discernment, and wisdom. Pick your friends carefully, and make sure they're safe and trustworthy people.

I have a very small and select circle of trusted friends who are in my corner no matter what. When we talk, the conversations are full of stuff that matters—with vulnerability a given. No holds barred and holding each other to a higher standard. *That* is what I would call unconditional love as well. And who doesn't want to have a bit of that to link up with vulnerability?

> **As iron sharpens iron, so a man sharpens the countenance of his friend.**
> **Proverbs 27:17 (NKJV)**

_____

_____

_____

_____

_____

_____

_____

_____

_____

_____

_____

_____

CIVIL DISCOURSE

Being taught to avoid talking about politics and religion has led to a lack of understanding of politics and religion. What we should have been taught was how to have a civil conversation about difficult subjects.

The operative word, which seems to have fallen out of use, is *civil*. Discussions, if they can even be called that, have gotten so nasty over recent years. Is there a better word to describe how people are talking about stuff now? Rants?

People voicing opposing views have been on the receiving end of condescension and screaming tirades of how stupid they are to hold such beliefs. They have been disrespected and belittled. It's little wonder that there are people who would prefer to keep their beliefs to themselves. Civil conversations have been few and far between.

_____

_____

_____

_____

_____

_____

_____

_____

A WHALE OF A TALE

A female humpback whale had become entangled in a spider web of crab traps and lines. She was weighted down by hundreds of pounds of traps that caused her to struggle to stay afloat. She also had hundreds of yards of line rope wrapped around her body, her tail, her torso, and a line tugging in her mouth.

This is her story of giving gratitude.

A fisherman spotted her just east of the Faralon Islands (outside the Golden Gate) and radioed for help. Within a few hours, the rescue team arrived and determined that she was so badly off, the only way to save her was to dive in and untangle her... a very dangerous proposition.

One slap with the tail could kill a rescuer.

They worked for hours with curved knives and eventually freed her.

When she was free, the divers say she swam in what seemed like joyful circles. She then came back to each and every diver, one at a time, nudged them, and pushed gently, thanking them. Some said it was the most incredibly beautiful experience of their lives.

The guy who cut the rope out of her mouth says her eye was following him the whole time, and he will never be the same.

May you be so fortunate to be surrounded by people who will help you get untangled from the things that are binding you.

And may you always know the joy of giving and receiving gratitude.

Practice gratitude frequently with those who have your back and are always in your corner no matter what.

_____
_____
_____
_____
_____
_____
_____
_____
_____
_____
_____
_____
_____
_____
_____
_____
_____
_____
_____
_____
_____
_____
_____
_____

In everything give thanks, for this is the will of God in Christ Jesus for you.
I Thessalonians 5:18 (NKJV)

ONE DAY LEFT

Sometimes I joke about what I'd do if I had one day left to live. Eat junk, go crazy, etc. Today it hit me: Jesus knew. And He washed feet.

Steve Bezner

SELAH... this is a thought-provoking post. If I knew that I was living my last day on earth, I'd be calling everyone who came to mind to let them know how much I loved and appreciated them. Plus, never wanting to leave anything unsaid, I would want to make sure that they had made the life-changing decision that would assure me that we would eventually be spending eternity together. How would *you* like to leave your life here when you relocate to your eternal home? We all have one, you know. Who wants to hear "Well done, good and faithful servant"? I do! This is my ultimate Public Service Announcement.

SAY "CHEESE"

Life is like a camera. Just focus on what's important.
Capture the good times. Develop from the negatives.
And if things don't work out... just take another shot.

Fill up your album with great adventures and safe, loving family and friends. There is so much that can be said about this analogy. First of all, determining what is important is—well—important. Life is short, even though it sometimes feels like it will never end. The older you get, the more you realize that your life here will be over before you know it. Figuring out what's really important and going after it with gusto is an adventure. Focus on the good times and take aim. Make sure to fit everything into your frame. Don't leave anything out.

Good times have a lot to do with *activities* and *people*. Zero in on making great memories. My personal favorite thing to do is spend lots of time with the people I love. It might involve travel or doing a work project or sharing a meal, but having a heartfelt, honest, and open conversation about things that matter is my idea of a really good time.

I learned a long time ago that life can be like a dark room where the negatives are developed. What starts out looking one way can develop into something looking quite the opposite. What an opportunity to make positive changes. It's never too late to take another shot for a better outcome. Pick yourself up, dust yourself off, and start all over again.

_____
_____
_____
_____
_____
_____
_____
_____
_____
_____
_____
_____
_____
_____
_____
_____
_____
_____
_____
_____
_____
_____
_____
_____

Seek first the kingdom of God and His righteousness, and all these things shall be added to you.
Matthew 6:33 (NKJV)

THE FOUR AGREEMENTS

Be Impeccable With Your Word

Speak with integrity. Say only what you mean. Avoid using the word to speak against yourself or to gossip about others. Use the power of your word in the direction of truth and love.

Don't Take Anything Personally

Nothing others do is because of you. What others say and do is a projection of their own reality, their own dream. When you are immune to the opinions and actions of others, you won't be the victim of needless suffering.

Don't Make Assumptions

Find the courage to ask questions and to express what you really want. Communicate with others as clearly as you can to avoid misunderstanding, sadness, and drama. With just this one agreement, you can completely transform your life.

Always Do Your Best

Your best is going to change from moment to moment; it will be different when you are healthy as opposed to sick. Under any circumstance, simply do your best, and you will avoid self-judgment, self-abuse, and regret.

Don Miguel Ruiz

Spiritual Warriors

These four agreements are implying that real connections are being made between two or more people. In a troubling trend, I am finding that some people are distancing themselves from making face-to-face—or even voice-to-voice—connections by choosing to communicate only via texts. It feels like an avoidant or even dismissive way to deal with others. So often a text can be written badly and convey a message that is completely misunderstood by the person receiving the message. It is difficult to address those misunderstandings very well without actually speaking to one another.

Assumptions, misunderstandings, offenses, and so much more can be quickly resolved if only we will risk bringing back the practice of real communication. This is my personal favorite way to connect and I'm sure you know that about me by now.

A DOUBLE WHAMMY!

The more chances you give someone, the less respect they'll start to have for you. They'll begin to ignore the standards that you've set because they'll know another chance will always be given. They're not afraid to lose you because they know, no matter what, you won't walk away. They get comfortable with depending on your forgiveness.

Never let a person get comfortable disrespecting you.

There are boundary busters—and then there are people who never even set boundaries at all. It's easy to be angry with people who are abusive and disrespectful. However, I have been irritated, perhaps even angry with people who are afraid to stand up against things like disrespect for a variety of reasons. Their excuses are they don't want to rock the boat, or they fear retaliation, or they are people-pleasers. By the way, just to be very clear, disrespectful people are *never* pleased by anything a people-pleaser does. Whatever the case may be, because a person who is disrespected doesn't use their voice to draw a line in the sand, not only do they lose the respect of the person who is playing them, they also lose the respect of those who observe what's going on. It's a *double whammy!*

People who learn how to set healthy boundaries and consistently enforce them become powerful and are admired by those who have prayed for them to enjoy a quality life filled with peace and joy. Living a life with self-respect *and* the respect of others is the best and a great goal. That, too, is a *double whammy!*

You don't make your words true by embellishing them with
religious lace. In making your speech sound more religious,
it becomes less true. Just say "yes" and "no." When you
manipulate words to get your own way, you go wrong.
Matthew 6:36-37 (MSG)

UNFORGIVENESS

I forgive people, but that doesn't mean I accept their behavior or trust them. I forgive them for me, so I can let go and move on with my life.

Love needs to be unconditional. It's a command, not a suggestion. Forgiveness, although difficult at times, is also a must. Respect and trust, on the other hand must be earned, but, when those two are missing, they aren't restored overnight. They must be earned back, and it takes a fair amount of time with the evidence of consistent changes of attitudes and behaviors. It's important to keep these relational elements straight. Plus, life is too short to get stuck in the anger, hurt, and bitterness cycle that winds up being residual pieces that accompany unforgiveness. Let the offenses go and learn to focus on and be thankful for the life you have. You only live once, so make the most of it. It is after all—eternal. No regrets!

_____

_____

_____

_____

_____

_____

_____

_____

_____

FRIENDSHIP

One day, all of us will get separated from each other. We will miss our conversations. Days, months, and years will pass until we rarely see each other. One day, our children will see our photos and ask, "Who are these people?" And we will smile with invisible tears and say,

"It was with them that I had the best days of my life."

I already dealt with my hundreds of loose photos by sorting them and sending them to new homes, for which my children are so thankful. When I relocate to Heaven, my children won't have to figure out who the people are in those pictures, because they have been distributed to where they belong. Even though I have handed out all my loose pictures, I still have plenty of photo albums for my children to look through though.

Here's the thing... my children have heard countless stories about the friends I have had over the years who filled me up and gave me the best days of my life. They will recognize most of the faces and remember the stories—and they will smile too.

WHOSE ASSIGNMENT IS IT?

God will never hold you responsible for someone else's assignment.

Steven Furtick

Since this is really a boundary issue, if you tend to enable others by doing their assignments for them, God may want to know why you have crossed the line and interfered with their growth process. *Stop it*! You're stunting their growth. Don't be a boundary buster!

_____

_____

_____

_____

_____

_____

_____

_____

_____

_____

_____

_____

_____

FAKE FRIENDSHIPS

The most dangerous creature on this earth is a fake friend.

Sometimes we miss the mark when we pick our friends. We tend to be drawn to people who are fun and have similar interests or belief systems, and that's understandable. Over time, we might begin to sense that something is amiss. We wonder what's going on. Flashing red lights become more intense. Those things that brought us together in the first place begin to lose their shine and importance. Over time, character issues begin to float to the surface. Outwardly the hugs may still be frequent, and conversations may still appear to be "friendly," but sincerity might be a missing component. The talks lack substance and authenticity. We need to be very careful when that happens.

There might be times when that "friend" begins to take potshots at us and even stab us in the back. Major betrayals, while still acting like a friend, are major trust busters. This is a dangerous connection, and there is no friendship of value anymore. There never was one that was real in the first place. It may have "looked" and "felt" good, but it never really was. We just missed the signs earlier on. That happens. When we begin to see things more clearly, we need to know when to walk away for our own safety.

Learn how to identify safe people, but learn how to be a safe person as well. It's a two-way street and involves something I call "teeter-totter reciprocity"—where give-and-take is equal and dependable. God's greatest desire for us is to enter a *real* friendship with Him *and* with other people. Healthy relationships are a high priority on God's list.

_____

_____

_____

_____

_____

_____

_____

_____

_____

_____

_____

_____

_____

_____

_____

_____

_____

_____

_____

_____

_____

_____

_____

_____

_____

A friend loves at all times, and a brother is born for a time of adversity.
Proverbs 17:17 (NIV)

THE TWO "EN" WORDS

It is not what you do for your children, but what you have taught them to do for themselves that will make them successful human beings.

Ann Landers

Doing for your kids is perfectly fine up to a point, but if it becomes easier to do everything for them and a habit is developed, two "en" words will be the "en"d result. We hear these words bandied about a lot these days. They are "enable" and "entitlement." When we use these words to describe our up-and-coming generation, perhaps we should take a good look in the mirror to find the real culprit—the "enabler" who created the problem in the first place—staring back at us.

I did it, but I'm so thankful for God's grace and for gaining a little bit of knowledge about what I was doing, so my ignorance on that subject didn't have any lasting effects on my kids. I made plenty of mistakes along the way, and I'm still working on doing a better job of observing the boundaries of others. By recognizing what needs to be done, I've had the desire to make necessary changes even now. I'm a firm believer in being a lifelong learner. My kids are adults now and are doing a fine job with figuring out how God intended for them to live their lives to the fullest. God is so good, and He had my back and helped me repair what I had messed up. It's never too late to mend what is broken.

Point your kids in the right direction ---
when they're old they won't be lost.
Proverbs 22:6 (MSG)

OFFENSE IS RUNNING RAMPANT

Our society strives to avoid any possibility of offending anyone... except GOD.

Billy Graham

Offending God is still a *big* problem, but people seem to be having no problem at all offending others over the past few years either. The empathy chip has lost its value. So much anger and hatred has divided families and friends, and the country is in turmoil.

The idea of "Come, let us reason together" has gone by the wayside. The claws are out, the rhetoric is vicious, and the attack is on. Civility appears to have become a lost art. All of it has caused great offense to God, and this sad situation will be a hard one to justify and explain away when the time comes. And make no mistake, the time is coming.

_____

_____

_____

_____

_____

_____

_____

_____

_____

OUT OF GAS

A relationship without trust is like a car without gas;

you can stay in it as long as you want,

but it still won't go anywhere.

You can always decide to buy a new car when the old one no longer serves its purpose, but even then, the new car will eventually run out of gas too. Relationships, perhaps more than anything else, need a lot of attention to work well. Make sure to keep up on required maintenance and top off the necessary levels that will keep everything running smoothly. The trust level is the most important thing to watch. If the red light comes on, don't ignore it. The relationship will fail if the trust level is sitting on empty.

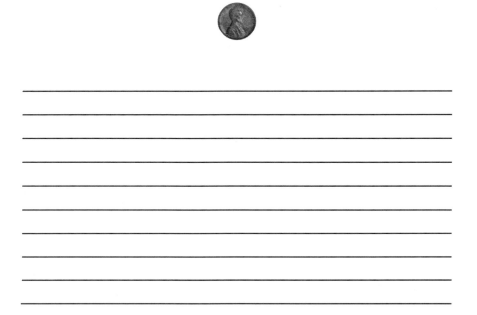

_____

_____

_____

_____

_____

_____

_____

_____

_____

DANGER!

The chief danger that confronts the coming century will be

Religion without the Holy Ghost,

Christianity without Christ,

Forgiveness without repentance,

Salvation without regeneration,

Politics without God,

Heaven without Hell.

William Booth

MAJOR TRUTH BOMB! Every single one of these points will make or break us, depending on how we respond to each danger. What are your thoughts on the effect and importance of each point?

_____

_____

_____

_____

_____

_____

_____

_____

AUTHENTIC CONNECTIONS

You can give a lot of yourself to others. You may be constantly helping people, but if it's all coming from you, it's not real connection. In order to connect, people must show up for you too.

Dr. Henry Cloud

The Power of the Other

Many people give a lot to others—sometimes more than that which is appropriate. When that happens, they can cross the line and become enablers. That creates many problems for both the enabler and the enabled. Often the giving and generous people have a hard time asking for and receiving what they need to fill up their love tank. Consequently, a safe, fulfilling, and real connection is incomplete.

Personal note: I used to be "the giver" and took a great deal of pride in being able to do for and give to others, all the while denying others the opportunity to give back to me. God had multiple chats with me about that. I was reminded that none of *my* giving would have been possible without His provision. It wasn't all about *me*; it was all about *Him!* Humility is a hard thing to come by when pride and arrogance are involved, but it was a lesson that I needed to learn. I haven't mastered it yet, but I'm getting better at learning how to be a recipient of blessings from others. If there is one thing I desire in life, it is to make full and complete loving and authentic connections with safe friends and family.

_____

_____

_____

_____

_____

_____

_____

_____

_____

_____

_____

_____

_____

_____

_____

_____

_____

_____

_____

_____

_____

_____

_____

**So let each one give as he purposes in his heart, not
grudgingly or of necessity; for God loves a cheerful giver.
II Corinthians 9:7 (NKJV)**

ACTIONS SPEAK LOUDER THAN WORDS

Young people eventually reveal by their actions if their motives are on the up and up.

Proverbs 20:11 (MSG)

On the other hand, when motives aren't noticeable, young people may just choose to go underground—nowhere to be found. When this happens, there might be a legitimate reason to be concerned. Sometimes young people who lack necessary life skills and problem-solving abilities are afraid of failure by doing the wrong thing—so they do nothing.

The fear of failure leads to shame. Rather than operating full of confidence with a tool belt full of what they need to get the job done well, their motives are all screwed up and not on the up and up. And, sadly, sometimes there is no motivation to do anything at all.

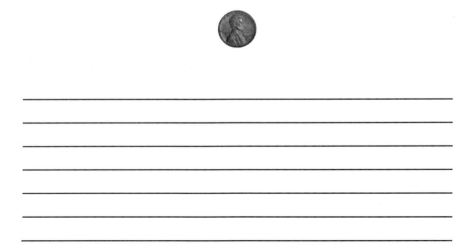

_____

_____

_____

_____

_____

_____

ACCOUNTABILITY ATTACKS

Being held accountable may feel like an attack if you're not ready to acknowledge how your poor decisions impact others.

Confrontation is never fun, especially when we're being called out on making poor choices. Sometimes it feels like we're being backed into a corner. We feel trapped—like *everybody* is picking on us. Then we look for ways to get away from the *attack*. It's been said that the best defense when confronted is a strong offense. We tend to push back, cry, kick, and scream as we try to justify our ill-advised decisions. On top of that, we feel victimized. That's a sure sign that we're not ready to take responsibility for our messes, and we hate it when anybody suggests that our actions and attitudes have affected and hurt others.

What we really need to do when this happens is count our blessings when someone cares enough about us to call us on our nonsense. It doesn't feel good, but if heeded, it turns out to be a good thing. An Empathy Chip begins to develop, and we begin to care about how our words or actions have hurt others. Taking a good, hard look at the decisions we've made and rectifying the situations is a great move toward growing up and becoming a responsible adult.

THE WISDOM OF SOLOMON

Two women were on a bus fighting bitterly over the last available seat.
The conductor had already tried unsuccessfully to intervene when the bus
driver shouted to the conductor, "Let the ugly one take the seat."
Both women stood for the rest of the journey.
Argument over! Case closed!

Sometimes there are no words. The passengers on the bus were a captive audience to escalating drama, and I'd say they got a good return on the price of their ticket to ride. It's hard to guess—did the driver's solution meet with stunned silence or a spontaneous outburst of uncontrollable laughter and applause? Kudos to the driver! He missed his calling. He should be wearing a long, black robe and wielding a gavel.

This scenario probably never happened in real life, but who knows? Life is funny, and bizarre behaviors in this crazy world are becoming commonplace, and common sense is not very common anymore. Common courtesy has fallen by the wayside too.

_____

_____

_____

_____

_____

_____

FRUIT INSPECTION

The Bible makes it clear that those who are genuinely saved are righteous and holy. They still sin, but with decreasing frequency. A believer hates his sin *(Romans 7:15-25)* and repents of it, hungering and thirsting for what is right. He obeys God, loves his brother, and hates the evil world system. No one can be a Christian and continue living the way he did before he knew Christ.

Defenders of the Gospel

We need more fruit inspectors who will take their job seriously and examine themselves first. Too many irregulars (or "bad apples") seem to be slipping into the mix. The time has come for those of us who claim to be Christians to hold ourselves to a higher standard. If we say we are a "Christian," we need to show the world what being a Christian really looks like. If we say we believe in God, we will live a life that shows Him honor and respect at all times. One foot in and one foot out doesn't get it anymore. If we *say* we are a Christian, we need to *be* one—for real. Let's do some self-inspection to see if we pass muster and will be seen by the world as the real deal.

ELECTRICAL SURGES

When two people relate to each other authentically and humanly, God is the electricity that surges between them.

Martin Buber

This is exactly how I feel when I spend time with friends and family who are open, honest, and vulnerable with me as I am with them; it is powerful and meaningful. I think this is what God wants—for us to be in fellowship with each other—encouraging, confronting, teaching, and loving one another. I believe He gets a real charge out of that!

But if we walk in the light as He is in the light, we have fellowship with one another, and the blood of Jesus Christ His Son cleanses us from all sin.
1 John 1:7 (NKJV)

_____

_____

_____

_____

_____

_____

_____

_____

_____

LOVING? NOT SO MUCH!

Codependency is driven by the agreement that I will work harder on your problem and your life than you do. This is not love.

LovingOnPurpose.com

An enabler may believe they are being kind and loving by assisting someone else with just about everything, but they're not. Instead, they are making it possible for the other person to stay stuck in a one-down position. The person being enabled begins to expect special treatment and develops a sense of entitlement. The cycle of codependency is complete at that point. A person who is being totally accommodated in their perceived helplessness by an enabler is never given the opportunity to grow up and take responsibility for their own life. This is *not* love!

PARENT ALERT

Children shouldn't have to sacrifice so that you can have the life you want. You make sacrifices so your children can have the life they deserve.

No child has ever been able to choose whether they want to be born into this world. Women who don't want to be bothered with the nuisance of raising a child they don't want end the pregnancy by getting an abortion. These days that's an easy thing to do and an entirely different discussion. Let it be said that I abhor abortion; it goes totally against God's will.

For the women who choose to become parents, whether planned or "accidental," your child is *not* an accident and no surprise to God. He has entrusted you with a precious child. Make sure you step up and meet their needs. Put aside your "what about me?" selfishness and help your child learn how to grow up well and have a great life. You won't be sorry—just do it. Their success will be your crowning glory for a job well done.

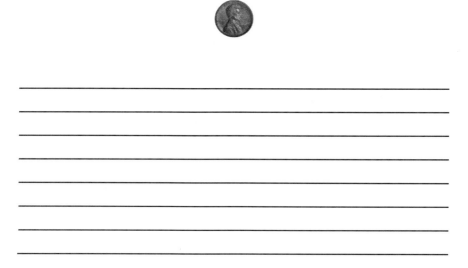

INTERNAL WOUNDS

Emotional abuse is just as damaging as physical abuse. The only difference between the two is with physical abuse you are wearing it on the outside for the world to see and the other is felt deep inside. Others cannot see the bruises on your heart.

Larry James

Words contain power! Whenever hurtful, hateful phrases are spoken to or about anybody, the damage is done. Once heard, these statements can be internalized and remain where they landed—in the mind and in the heart. Without treatment administered by trained specialists or surrendered to Jesus' healing touch, the wounds can fester and affect how that person functions in life.

> **A word out of your mouth may seem of no account, but it can accomplish nearly anything... or destroy it.**
> **James 3:5 (MSG)**

Walking wounded people without outward signs of injury are everywhere. Sometimes internal wounds are manifested in outward behaviors and attitudes. It may be apparent to others that something is wrong, but there are no outward marks to validate their suspicions unless the wounded person is willing to talk about their pain. In many ways, emotional abuse is more damaging than physical abuse and takes much longer to heal. As my mom used to say, *"Watch your mouth!"*

We must deliberately be kind.

Let the words of my mouth and the meditation of my heart
be acceptable in Your sight, O Lord, my strength and my
Redeemer.
Psalm 19:14 (NKJV)

THE LONGEVITY FACTOR

Very interestingly, after twenty years of research and practice as a cardiologist, Ornish wrote in his book, *Love and Survival*, that no other factor in medicine, "not diet, not smoking, not exercise, not stress, not genetics, not drugs, not surgery," affects our health, quality and length of life more than feeling loved and cared for.

D r. Dean Ornish got it right on the money. God's plan for fulfilling and healthy lives involves *relationships*—vertical with Him first—and horizontal with others second. Face-to-face is essential. Don't think for a minute that Facebook or other technical devices will suffice. That is often man's plan, but not God's.

For as long as I live, I will seek out people who are like-minded. My goal is to love and be loved. When that happens, life has great value and an even greater purpose. Sharing God's love and caring for others is probably my highest calling. If connecting with others well is the longevity component, I am probably destined to live a long and productive life. When I told my friend, Kelly, about what was determined to be the key to a long life, namely, being in great relationships with others—she turned to me and said, "You're going to live FOREVER!" And she's right! I will! My physical life will come to an end at some point, but I will live forever—here *and* in Heaven.

_____

_____

_____

_____

_____

_____

_____

_____

_____

_____

_____

_____

_____

_____

_____

_____

_____

_____

_____

_____

_____

_____

You shall walk in all the ways which the LORD your God has
commanded you, that you may live and *that it may be* well
with you, and *that* you may prolong *your* days in the land
which you shall possess.
Deuteronomy 5:33 (NKJV)

APOLOGIES CAN BE DISMISSIVE

Apologies don't mean anything if you keep doing what you're sorry for.

Dr. Laura

For those who dismiss people with a quick apology, save your breath. The ones you have hurt or offended would much rather you get some insight, do some hard work, and change the behaviors that keep calling for a need to apologize—*again*. Whatever you're doing that warrants frequent apologies needs to stop. The recipients of your meaningless and frequent words of apology are not impressed with just a "sorry" anymore. They've heard it before, and it doesn't mean a thing. They would be ecstatic if changed behaviors and attitudes would actually match the message that is supposed to be conveyed by the meaning of the word "sorry." When there is a sense of heartfelt, genuine regret, it's more likely that change is on the horizon.

ONE THING OF GREAT VALUE TO ME

I think that when the dust settles,
we will realize how very little we need,
how very much we actually have,
and the true value of human connection.

I look around at every *thing* I have and wonder about how much of it I really need. I've gone through two major purging events over the last sixteen years when I made two big moves. As my time is winding down—like a snowball gains momentum rolling downhill—I still discover things that don't hold as much interest or value to me, so I continue sorting[1].

The one thing that I hold dearest in life is the ability to make human connections that feed my heart and soul. Without that, my life would lose its luster. I intend to keep shining all the rest of my days.

_____

_____

_____

_____

[1]*My mom was a big "sorter." Genetics tell me I came by it honestly.*

SHIFTING ROLES

I wish you were home with me,
where I can see you and hug you and keep you safe.
Sincerely,
Moms of grown kids everywhere

I read this and immediately flipped it. I wonder how many parents who are older would like to be with their children because their grown kids would give *them* a sense of security and being loved well. There may come a time when the older parent begins to have uncertainties about the challenges they are facing. The roles may switch. I can feel it making a shift in my own life, and my kids are stepping up and addressing the spaces that need reassurance.

This brings back memories for me. I can certainly remember when I, the grown "child," became my mom's safety net. Whatever the case may be, I believe we all long to be together and will cherish the time when it can happen again.

BURNING BRIDGES

Sometimes burning bridges isn't a bad thing. It prevents you from going back to a place you should never have been in the first place.

The Savvy Sistah.com

A box of matches is not very expensive, but staying in a toxic, abusive, and destructive relationship can be very costly. It might even be way more than you can afford—it could cost you your life. There are relationships that have been in crash-and-burn mode for a long time. Having the courage to pack up and walk away—or run—is way past due. The life you save may be your own.

_____
_____
_____
_____
_____
_____
_____
_____
_____
_____
_____

CRITICAL THINKING

Criticism is a misuse of my authority.

Bill Johnson

Bill Johnson is the senior leader of Bethel Church in Redding, California and is a well-known minister and evangelist. When my friend, Christina, saw this post, she commented, "Should I critique this? Constructive criticism is therapeutic and healing when used correctly."

I agreed with Christina. The verses in Proverbs about "iron sharpening iron" and "the wounds of a friend," as well as in other places in the Bible, tell us to confront others when we observe things are a little off. Is that criticism? It *can* be done lovingly and bring healing and growth. After looking for synonyms of the word criticism, I went to the Word to search for verses about reproof and correction. It seemed to me that Johnson's post called for further investigation—a search for Scripture to balance Scripture. Christina further said, "As good parents, we guide our children into righteousness. It doesn't just happen through osmosis."

When people get offended and feel like they're being judged and harshly criticized, they may be reacting to hurtful memories from their past experiences. One of my old classmates just about came out of her chair at one of my group sessions when I mentioned constructive criticism. She loudly declared that there was *nothing* constructive about criticism. She grew up with a very critical mother who, by her report, never approved of anything she ever did. No amount of discussion or references to verses about correction or reproof changed her mind. She still viewed it as criticism, and she wasn't about to change her mind about that subject. Case closed!

When I'm confronted, it sometimes *feels* judgmental and critical. That's when I need to step back and look at the heart of the one confronting me. If I trust them and their love and concern for me, I listen and respond. After all, God confronts and reproves me all the time, and He *really* loves me and has my best interest at heart. I choose to believe that my safe friends mean me no harm when they care enough to call me on my bad behaviors. Life is too short to waste my time on being offended, especially when the criticism will result in my making the corrections needed to become all I was created to be.

GRANDMAS

If you were blessed to know your grandma...
what was the one thing that you remember most about her?

My mom's mother relocated to Heaven before I was born, but I learned plenty about her character, integrity, and unconditional love by the way my mom and her siblings lived their lives. My grandma was a great role model, and they learned from her. It's true that what goes on in the home is passed on to the children. My grandma loved the Lord, practiced hospitality, and loved everybody extravagantly. I'm looking forward to meeting her one day. Her legacy lived on through her children, and they followed her example. Now they have all joined her and are having the time of their lives. My siblings, cousins, and I have been left to carry on and perpetuate her legacy—*big shoes to fill.*

_____

_____

_____

_____

_____

_____

_____

_____

_____

MATCHING WORDS WITH ACTIONS

The attitude that you have as a parent is what your kids will learn from, more than what you tell them. They don't remember what you try to teach them. They remember what you are.

Jim Henson

Something to remember when your words of scolding and instruction don't match your own conduct or behavior. If you say it, live it! What you have decided is best for your kids must be best for you as well. It's true that it is your responsibility to be an excellent caretaker of your kids. It's a daunting job at times for sure. It is ever so much more important to take good care of yourself first—your conduct, your values, and your priorities. Studies have shown, in most cases, that kids grow up to mimic the way they observed the behaviors in their homes. They may even have heard "do as I say, not as I do" a million times, but those words fall on deaf ears. If whatever is allowed to go on is good enough for the parent, it's good enough for them too. What goes on in the home is actively *taught* to the kids. Power up to parent well.

Andy Andrews has said that the goal isn't to have good kids; the goal is to raise great adults. The way to do that is to be a great adult in the presence of your kids. They will learn from the example you set. If the parent falls down on the job, their kids will either live the same way their parents did or they will get the help they need to become great adults from somebody else later on when they are out on their own. How nice it would be for parents to step up and get the job done well from day one.

_____
_____
_____
_____
_____
_____
_____
_____
_____
_____
_____
_____
_____
_____
_____
_____
_____
_____
_____
_____

Parents rejoice when their children turn out well; wise
children become proud parents. So make your father happy!
Make your mother proud! Dear child, I want your full
attention; please do what I show you.
Proverbs 22:24-26 (MSG)

LACK OF BOUNDARIES

It's not a good thing to be a person without consistent limits, thinking you just want to be nice and please everybody and not "make" anybody mad at you. Keeping the "peace at any price" idea, as my dad used to say, can be very costly. And it is a false peace. Invariably, people wind up walking all over those of you who don't have the courage to grow a backbone and develop boundaries by using the simple word "No." Perhaps you might even believe you don't have a right to challenge your controllers. Consequently, you just might become a *narcissist magnet*. And that, my friend, results in situations that lack R-E-S-P-E-C-T, big time.

Do everyone a big favor and let your "Yes" really mean yes and your "No" really mean no. That way, as a boundary-setter, you will properly mature and become all you were created to be. Not everyone will be thrilled to be on the receiving end of your decision to take back control of your own life, but *tough toenails!*

It is, after all, *your life!*

Rowgo

C an you tell that I'm passionate about boundaries? They lead to *freedom* and *safety* as you develop into the person you were created to be. God was the originator of boundaries, and He observes and keeps them—*always*. There was a time I struggled at making and keeping boundaries because I didn't really understand how important they were or how to develop them or even how they could be incredibly beneficial to my quality of life. Over many years of hit-and-miss attempts, I have seen improvement.

My recommended reading for those of you who struggle in this area and didn't even know there was such a thing as a boundary is the book, *Boundaries*, by Dr. Henry Cloud and Dr. John Townsend. They have also written additional Boundaries books that pinpoint specific areas and groups. They are priceless and a great way to regain your sanity and life if you begin to practice what they teach. Gain self-respect and refuse being disrespected by others. Build your fence and put up your "No Trespassing" sign. Enough is enough, or as my daughter, Mara, says, "Enough is too much!"

MEAN PEOPLE

Mean people don't bother me a bit.

Mean people who disguise themselves as nice people bother me a whole lot.

Soul Quest

This is an insidious element of unsafe people and often not very easy to spot. This tends to show up very subtly in passive-aggressive behaviors, which have a very real element of meanness at the core. Mean people may be able to cover up their real selves and hide behind their masks for a while, but eventually their true character will seep out and show their real colors. This is a bona fide betrayal and trust buster and it hurts like fury. Be on guard and learn how to spot the flashing red lights.

_____

_____

_____

_____

_____

_____

_____

_____

_____

YOU CAN'T MAKE ME

Being single and having peace of mind is better than being with someone who makes you feel like your mind is in pieces.

Bryan Burden

NEWFLASH! Nobody can *make you* feel anything, but toxic, unsafe people can certainly have a negative effect on one's peace of mind. I really dislike hearing "They made me _____ (fill in the blank)" statements. Giving away personal power and not taking responsibility for attitudes, emotional reactions and behaviors is a boundary problem that irritates me no end. It is absolutely time to take personal ownership of these essential areas.

_____

_____

_____

_____

_____

_____

_____

_____

_____

_____

SIGNS OF A TOXIC PERSON

Nothing you can say or do is good enough.

They comment on the smallest flaw or perceived imperfection.

They drag up your past and won't allow you to be different.

They leave you feeling guilty and ashamed of who you are.

They're critical, controlling, and don't think about your needs.

They leave you feeling beaten, wounded, battered, bruised and torn.

They violate your boundaries, and they never respect "no."

They don't care about your feelings and like to see you suffer.

It's always about them and what they think and want and feel.

B e vigilant. Take time to make a valid and accurate identification when entering into *all* relationships. Develop and follow carefully devised boundaries and search for safe people to welcome into your life.

_____

_____

_____

_____

_____

_____

_____

_____

YOU ARE NOT EVERYONE'S CUP OF TEA

The world is filled with people who, no matter what you do, no matter what you try, will simply not like you. But the world is also filled with those who love you fiercely. The ones who love you: they are YOUR people. Don't waste your finite time and heart trying to convince the people who aren't your people that you have value. They will miss it completely. They won't buy what you are selling.

Don't try to convince them to walk your path with you, because you will only waste your time and your emotional good health. You are not for them, and they are not for you. You are not their cup of tea, and they are not yours. Politely wave them along and you move away as well. Seek to share your path with those who recognize your gifts—who you are. Be who you are.

You are not everyone's cup of tea, and that is OK.

If you were to throw a tea party, who would you invite and who would come? I know who would be at the top of my list every time, and He would *always* show up. He really loves me! Over the years, I have worked very diligently on learning how to be a safe and trustworthy friend to others, so I'm aware of who the people in my life are who are happy to call me their friend. I am their cup of tea, and they are mine as well.

_____
_____
_____
_____
_____
_____
_____
_____
_____
_____
_____
_____
_____
_____
_____
_____
_____
_____
_____
_____
_____
_____
_____
_____

Then Jesus said to him, "A certain man gave a great supper
and invited many, and sent his servant at supper time to say
to those who were invited, 'Come, for all things are now
ready.' But they all with one accord began to make excuses."
Luke 14:16-18b (NKJV)

3

FOCUSED UPWARD

THE PRICE OF A DONUT

There was a certain Professor of Religion named Dr. Christianson who taught at a small college in the Western United States. Dr. Christianson taught the required survey course in Christianity at this particular institution. Every student was required to take this course his or her freshman year regardless of his or her major. Although Dr. Christianson tried hard to communicate the essence of the gospel in his class, he found that most of his students looked upon the course as nothing but required drudgery. Despite his best efforts, most students refused to take Christianity seriously.

This year, Dr. Christianson had a special student named Steve. Steve was only a freshman but was studying with the intent of going on to seminary for the ministry. Steve was popular, he was well-liked, and he was an imposing physical specimen. He was now the starting center on the school football team and was the best student in the professor's class.

One day, Dr. Christianson asked Steve to stay after class so he could talk with him. "How many pushups can you do?

Steve said, "I do about 200 every night."

"200? That's pretty good, Steve," Dr. Christianson said. "Do you think you could do 300?"

Steve replied, "I don't know... I've never done 300 at a time."

"Do you think you could?" again asked Dr. Christianson.

"Well, I can try," said Steve

"Can you do 300 in sets of 10? I have a class project in mind, and I need you to do about 300 pushups in sets of ten for this to work. Can you do it? I need you to tell me you can do it," said the professor.

Steve said, "Well... I think I can... yeah, I can do it."

Dr. Christianson said, "Good! I need you to do this on Friday. Let me explain what I have in mind."

Friday came, and Steve got to class early and sat in the front of the room. When class started, the professor pulled out a big box of donuts. These weren't the normal kinds of donuts; they were the extra fancy BIG kind with cream centers and frosting swirls.

Everyone was pretty excited it was Friday, the last class of the day, and they were going to get an early start on the weekend with a party in Dr. Christianson's class.

Dr. Christianson went to the first girl in the first row and asked, "Cynthia, do you want to have one of these donuts?"

Cynthia said, "Yes."

Dr. Christianson then turned to Steve and asked, "Steve, would you do ten pushups so that Cynthia can have a donut?"

"Sure." Steve jumped down from his desk to do a quick ten. Then Steve again sat in his desk. Dr. Christianson put a donut on Cynthia's desk.

Dr. Christianson then went to Joe, the next person, and asked, "Joe, do you want a donut?"

Joe said, "Yes."

Dr. Christianson asked, "Steve, would you do ten pushups so Joe can have a donut?" Steve did ten pushups, and Joe got a donut.

And so it went, down the first aisle, Steve did ten pushups for every person before they got their donut, and down the second aisle, until Dr. Christianson came to Scott. Scott was on the basketball team and in as good condition as Steve. He was very popular and never lacking for female companionship. When the professor asked, "Scott, do you want a donut?"

Scott's reply was, "Well, can I do my own pushups?"

Dr. Christianson said, "No, Steve has to do them."

Then Scott said, "Well, I don't want one then."

Dr. Christianson shrugged and then turned to Steve and asked, "Steve, would you do ten pushups so Scott can have a donut he doesn't want?" With perfect obedience, Steve started to do ten pushups.

Scott said, "HEY! I said I didn't want one!"

Dr. Christianson said, "Look...this is my classroom, my class, my desks, and these are my donuts. Just leave it on the desk if you don't want it." And he put a donut on Scott's desk.

Now by this time, Steve had begun to slow down a little. He just stayed on the floor between sets because it took too much effort to be getting up and down. You could start to see a little perspiration coming out around his brow. Dr. Christianson started down the third row. Now the students were beginning to get a little angry.

Dr. Christianson asked Jenny, "Jenny, do you want a donut?"

Sternly, Jenny said, "No." Then Dr. Christianson asked Steve, "Steve, would you do ten more pushups so Jenny can have a donut that she doesn't want?" Steve did ten, and Jenny got a donut.

By now, a growing sense of uneasiness filled the room. The students were beginning to say "No," and there were all these uneaten donuts on the desks. Steve also had to really put forth a lot of extra effort to get these pushups done for each donut. There began to be a small pool of sweat on the floor beneath his face. His arms and brow were beginning to get red because of the physical effort involved.

Dr. Christianson started down the fourth row.

During his class, however, some students from other classes had wandered in and sat down on the steps along the radiators that ran down the side of the room. When the professor realized this, he did a quick count and saw that now there were 34 students in the room.

He started to worry if Steve would be able to make it.

Dr. Christianson went on to the next person and the next and the next. Near the end of that row, Steve was really having a rough time. He was taking a lot more time to complete each set.

A few moments later, Jason, a recent transfer student, came to the room and was about to come in when all the students yelled in one voice, "NO! Don't come in! Stay out!" Jason didn't know what was going on.

Steve picked up his head and said, "No, let him come."

Dr. Christianson said, "You realize that if Jason comes in, you will have to do ten pushups for him?"

Steve said, "Yes, let him come in. Give him a donut."

Dr. Christianson said "Okay, Steve, I'll let you get Jason's out of the way right now. Jason, do you want a donut?" Jason, new to the room, hardly knew what was going on.

"Yes," he said, "give me a donut."

"Steve, will you do ten pushups so that Jason can have a donut?" Steve did ten pushups very slowly and with great effort. Jason, bewildered, was handed a donut and sat down.

Dr. Christianson finished the fourth row, and then started on those visitors seated by the heaters. Steve's arms were now shaking with each pushup in a struggle to lift himself against the force of gravity. Sweat was profusely dropping off of his face and, by this time, there was no sound except his heavy breathing. There was not a dry eye in the room.

The very last two students in the room were two young women, both cheerleaders, and very popular. Dr. Christianson went to Linda, the second to last and asked, "Linda, do you want a donut?"

Linda said, very sadly, "No, thank you."

Dr. Christianson quietly asked, "Steve, would you do ten pushups so that Linda can have a donut she doesn't want?" Grunting from the effort, Steve did ten very slow pushups for Linda.

Then Dr. Christianson turned to the last girl, Susan. "Susan, do you want a donut?"

Susan, with tears flowing down her face, she began to cry. "Dr. Christianson, why can't I help him?"

Dr. Christianson, with tears of his own, said, "No, Steve has to do it alone. I have given him this task, and he is in charge of seeing that everyone has an opportunity for a donut whether they want it or not.

When I decided to have a party this last day of class, I looked at my gradebook. Steve is the only student with a perfect grade. Everyone else has failed a test, skipped class, or offered me inferior work.

Steve told me that when a player messes up in football practice, he must do pushups. I told Steve that none of you could come to my party unless he paid the price by doing your pushups. He and I made a deal for your sakes.

Steve, would you do ten pushups so Susan can have a donut?"

As Steve very slowly finished his last pushup, with the understanding that he had accomplished all that was required of him, having done 350 pushups, his arms buckled beneath him and he fell to the floor.

Dr. Christianson turned to the room and said, "And so it was, that our Savior, Jesus Christ, on the cross, pled to the Father, 'into thy hands I commend my spirit.' With the understanding that He had done everything that was required of Him, He yielded up His life. And like some of those in this room, many of us leave the gift on the desk, uneaten."

Two students helped Steve up off the floor and to a seat, physically exhausted, but wearing a thin smile. "Well done, good and faithful servant," said the professor, adding, "Not all sermons are preached in words."

Turning to his class, the professor said, "My wish is that you might understand and fully comprehend all the riches of grace and mercy that have been given to you through the sacrifice of our Lord and Savior Jesus Christ for us all, now and forever. Whether or not we choose to accept His gift to us, the price has been paid. Wouldn't you be foolish and ungrateful to leave it laying on the desk?"

AUTHOR UNKNOWN

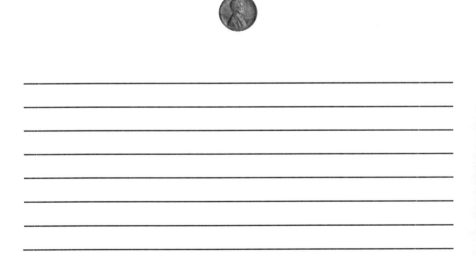

_____

_____

_____

_____

_____

_____

_____

KEEP THE MAIN THING THE MAIN THING

Growing in your relationship with God, every day should be your main priority.
If you do that, He will take care of everything else

I've heard it said that it's all about who you know. If you want that advantage or edge to get ahead and be successful in this life, be sure to surround yourself with trustworthy, safe people. But the very best place to start is to enter a real and committed relationship with the One who got everything started in the first place. It really *is* all about who you know.

_____

_____

_____

_____

_____

_____

_____

_____

_____

_____

_____

_____

_____

WHEN A MAN LOVES A WOMAN

Only when a man looks to JESUS, does a man know how to treat a woman.

Ann Voskamp

This is the kind of counsel, encouragement, and instruction we need to pass on to our sons, grandsons and, yes, even our great-grandsons—if we are blessed to live that long. So, it's very important to train them up in the way they really need to go, so that they will enjoy the one life that has been given to them.

Point your kids in the right direction—when they're old they won't be lost.
Proverbs 22:6 (MSG)

Of course, that means that we must have a clue about the whole procedure as well.

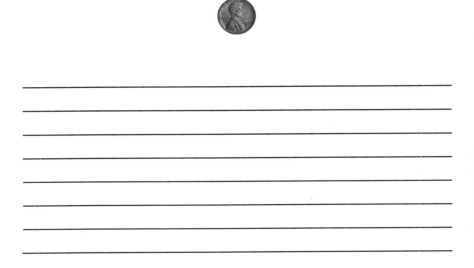

_____

_____

_____

_____

_____

_____

_____

I LOVE THIS ANALOGY

When GOD wanted to create fish, HE spoke to the sea. When GOD wanted to create trees, HE spoke to the earth. BUT when GOD wanted to create man, HE turned to Himself.

Then GOD said: "Let us make man in our image and in our likeness."

Note: If you take a fish out of the water, it will die; and when you remove a tree from soil, it will also die.

Likewise, when man is disconnected from GOD, he dies. GOD is our natural environment. We were created to live in His presence. We have to be connected to Him because it is only in Him that life exists.

Let's stay connected to GOD.

We recall that water without fish is still water, but fish without water is nothing. The soil without a tree is still soil, but the tree without soil is nothing. GOD without man is still GOD, but man without GOD is nothing.

No matter how I scrutinize this analogy, I can't figure out a way to dispute it. Maybe it's because I've spent so many years getting to know my Creator.

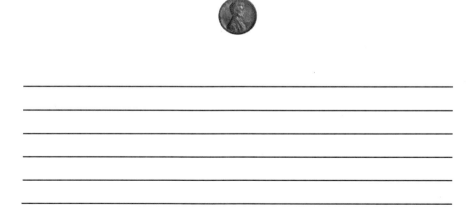

_____

_____

_____

_____

_____

_____

GRADE GOALS

You cannot pray for an A and study for a B. You cannot pray for a faithful relationship and still live an unfaithful life. Moral of the story is you cannot pray for something and act less. Don't question my God and His abilities when your actions don't match your prayers.

This is an "if-then" scenario. Don't ask God to deliver on anything if you are not willing to honor Him with your whole heart. If you know the right thing to do and don't do it, it isn't an "oops" or "my bad." James 4:17 calls it what it is—*sin*. God doesn't operate like the lottery, it's not a crap shoot with Him. His promises are yes and amen, but you must do it His way.

Here's the deal though—everyone is free to pray for whatever they want—however they want. So, you *can* pray for an A with only a B effort, but you will most likely still wind up with a B. My prayer would be that the B student doesn't wind up blaming God for not answering their misguided prayer. Every test that you face in life will take time and call for tough choices to be made. Taking responsible actions by diligently working hard to achieve goals will show how willing you are to go after the A.

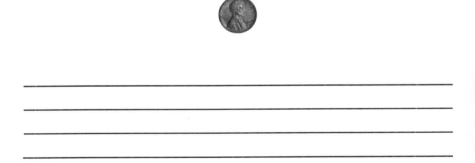

_____

_____

_____

_____

GOD-PLEASERS

Decisions become easier when your will to please God outweighs your will to please the world.

MyBible.com

This is true but pleasing God over and above jumping through hoops and trying to please *certain people*—forget about the whole world—is a whole different can of worms. Some people tend to be irritated with you if you don't do what they want you to do, because they disdainfully view you as "one of those God-pleasers." They tend to think you're way too "religious" and carrying this "Jesus stuff" too far. My thoughts? I will always try to lean toward making decisions that please God—and *those decisions* are so much easier to make because the Instructions are crystal clear.

LET IT GO

If it stops you from getting closer to God,

then it needs to go.

J C L U   F O R E V E R

WHATever or WHOever *it* is! You get to decide whether getting closer to God is a matter of high priority in your life though. Maybe it isn't, but the consequences of *your* choices will be on you then.

_____

_____

_____

_____

_____

_____

_____

_____

_____

_____

_____

_____

_____

MAP APPS

Life isn't about finding yourself...

it's about discovering who God created you to be.

This is an important distinction. These days, we have difficulty getting anywhere without a map app. Use the Godly Positional System (GPS). He always knows where you are and where you need to go.

_____

_____

_____

_____

_____

_____

_____

_____

_____

_____

_____

_____

_____

_____

_____

_____

IF I ONLY HAD A BRAIN

Brains are awesome...
I wish everybody had one.

Here's the deal... *everybody* has a brain, but not everybody has learned how to use it properly. The Instruction Manual is called the Bible, and it is written by the Creator of all life—which includes the brain. It's time to renew your mind. Here's a clear explanation, found in The Message, of how to do this:

So here's what I want you to do, God helping you:
Take your everyday, ordinary life—your sleeping, eating,
going-to-work, and walking-around life—and place it before
God as an offering. Embracing what God does for you is the
best thing you can do for Him.
Don't become so well-adjusted to your culture that you fit
into it without even thinking. Instead, fix your attention on
God. You'll be changed from the inside out. Readily
recognize what He wants from you, and quickly respond to
it.
Unlike the culture around you, always dragging you down to
its level of immaturity, God brings the best out of you,
develops well-formed maturity in you...
Romans 12:1,2 (MSG)

These two verses are among my favorite verses in the Bible. They remind me that I continually must think about what I am thinking about. When I do that, I should also think about *how* I'm thinking about things. Because my thoughts sometimes go a little wacky, I am continually renewing my mind to straighten out and change my big ideas. I don't have all the answers, but I know who does. And I plan to always consult with Him.

God gifted me with a brain, and He is always ready to show me how to use it in a way that brings Him honor and respect. When I line up my thought processes and begin to think the way that God thinks, I am content.

_____

_____

_____

_____

_____

_____

_____

_____

_____

_____

_____

_____

_____

_____

_____

_____

_____

_____

_____

WHO IS IN CONTROL?

God is in control!
But He doesn't expect you to lean on a shovel and pray for a hole.

Teamwork and reciprocity—you do your part—God will do His. Too often we behave like entitled children and bark out orders to God. And then we have the audacity to call it prayer. God, in His infinite wisdom, has given us things to do too. He much prefers to be yoked together with us as we experience our walk through life with Him.

_____

_____

_____

_____

_____

_____

_____

_____

_____

_____

_____

_____

CALL IT WHAT IT IS

GRACE is when God gives us good things that we don't deserve

MERCY is when He spares us from bad things we deserve

BLESSINGS are when He is generous with both

Truly, we can never run out of reasons to thank Him

God is good all the time!

These definitions are very clear and our response should also be loud and very clear—*thankful!*

_____

_____

_____

_____

_____

_____

_____

_____

_____

_____

_____

_____

TRAIL MIX

The Bible is not a bag of trail mix.
You can't just pick out the pieces you like and ignore the rest.

Some of it is hard to chew on and swallow but embracing and putting the whole thing to use is necessary in order to have a balanced diet and good health.

All Scripture is God-breathed and is useful for teaching, rebuking, correcting and training in righteousness, so that the servant of God may be thoroughly equipped for every good work.
2 Timothy 3:16-17

_____
_____
_____
_____
_____
_____
_____
_____
_____
_____
_____

A RANGE OF AUTHORITY

Do we, as believers, have authority over Satan and demons and sickness? Well, it depends what you mean by that question.

Can you resist Satan yourself if he tempts you? Yes

Can you resist Satan if he tries to devour you? Yes

Can you quench, with the shield of faith, every fiery javelin of the wicked one launched at you? Yes

Can you cast demons out of others if they truly want to be set free? Yes

Can you lay hands on a sick person and they will recover? Yes

But – Can you command Satan to never tempt another person on the planet? No

But – Can you bind the work of every demon in your city? No

But – Can you pronounce a global judgment on a virus commanding it to never exist on the earth anymore? No

Friends... there is a Range of Authority we have as believers. And we need to know what that range of authority is. It is not unlimited, no matter how much we wish it was or act like it is.

We also have to understand things like the manifestation of the Spirit. If a gift of faith is in operation through a believer or a working of miracles in manifestation, then by the power and working of the Holy Spirit, believers can accomplish things far beyond their own faith and beyond their general range of authority as a believer.

So...

Be Full of Faith

Believe God

Be Bold

Pray with Passion

Take your place as a New Covenant Believer

Exercise your Authority

But – be sound in your spiritual understanding and don't try to operate beyond your True Range of Authority.

Guy Duininck

We, as Christians, have a range of authority. As Guy Duininck says, it's important to know and understand what falls within our range and what doesn't. Too many people are trying to operate without a valid license.

_____
_____
_____
_____
_____
_____
_____
_____
_____
_____
_____
_____
_____
_____
_____
_____
_____

WRITE THIS DOWN!

Life without God is like an unsharpened pencil...

there is no point.

Time to get the lead out and live the life that has a point to it! God has given us very clear instructions on how to live a fulfilling, purposeful life. It gets off to a very good start when we pay careful attention and obey His first and most important commandment.

And you shall love the Lord your God with all your heart, with all your soul, with all your mind, and with all your strength. This *is* the first commandment.
Mark 12:30 (NKJV)

_____

_____

_____

_____

_____

_____

_____

_____

_____

_____

_____

_____

I'M NOT DOWN YET

Flowers grow back, even after they are stepped on.

So will I.

Bouncing back despite adversity brought about by people or circumstances brings honor to the One who has already established a plan for my life. I may be down, but I'm not out. Might as well rise to the challenge and grow back stronger.

Greater is He that is in you than he that is in the world.
I John 4:4b (KJV)

THE ULTIMATE DESIRE OF MY HEART

There is nothing that a Christian mother wants more than to spend all of eternity with her children.

I heard my mom say this more than once. Now it is on my mind and embedded in my heart daily, but it extends to my grandchildren, my great-grands, and my friends as well. As my day of relocation draws closer, I have become quite vocal about this subject. God doesn't want anyone to perish and miss out on spending eternity with Him. *Neither do I!*

C'mon, y'all... let's party! There is no pandemic there. No social distancing and definitely no masks. We will be seen as we are.

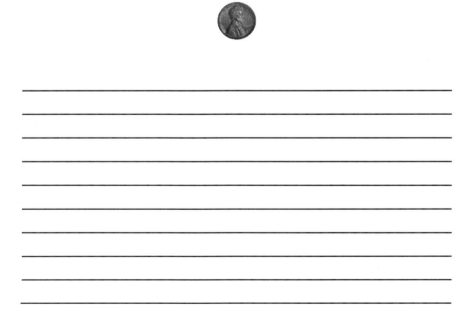

LIFETIME GUARANTEE

Duct tape may patch a lot of things,

but three nails fixed everything!

Few people are checking themselves into the shop for total repairs and restoration, even though everyone has been given the opportunity for a radical "do over." If everyone takes the time to do a "cross" check of what's needed to fix everything, three nails will prove to be more than adequate to get the job done.

_____

_____

_____

_____

_____

_____

_____

_____

_____

_____

_____

_____

IF-THEN

Ephesians 3:20 showed up on Facebook. Almost all of it was underlined.

<u>God will do exceedingly, abundantly above all that I ask or think.</u> Because I honor Him, <u>His blessings will chase me down and overtake me. I will be in the right place at the right time. People will go out of their way to be good to me. I am surrounded by God's favor.</u> <u>This is my declaration.</u>

Joel Osteen

The key to this passage is what is *not* underlined. I wonder why. This looks like an "If-then" verse. *If* we will *honor God, then* the rest will follow. It's amazing how often we grab bits and pieces of verses that benefit us and suit our purposes and desires but leave out the parts that require personal responsibility and action on our part. We *do* have *response-ability*, you know. Our relationship with God, if we are fully committed and want the best outcome, requires reciprocity.

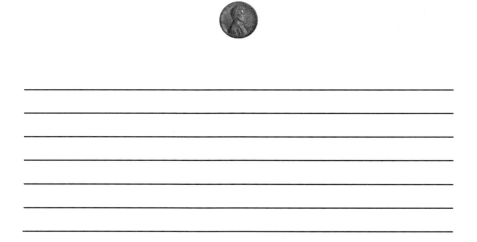

DISCIPLINE

In Matthew 4:4, Jesus said:

Man shall not live by bread alone, but by every word that proceeds from the mouth of God.

In other words,

don't trust your feelings,

don't trust your wishes,

don't trust your understanding,

go by the Word of God.

Discipline yourself not to be motivated by anything that isn't the Word of God.

Derek Prince

This is a great word for what seems to be going on these days. People appear to be running on whims and strong opinions and adrenaline and emotions in just about every situation, large and small. Political, spiritual, relational—you name it. Returning to the authentic Instruction Manual and following directions would restore peace, stability, and reason. As for me? I'm all in for following God's wise counsel and direction for my life. My own big ideas, opinions, and feelings have been less than helpful at times and have led me straight to dead ends. I'm paying attention to my Godly Positional System (GPS), so I can arrive at my appointed destination.

_____

_____

_____

_____

_____

_____

_____

_____

_____

_____

_____

_____

_____

_____

_____

_____

_____

_____

_____

_____

_____

_____

_____

_____

**Every word of God is pure; He is a shield to those who put
their trust in Him.
Proverbs 30:5 (NKJV)**

THE INFORMER

If you don't read the newspaper, you are uninformed.

If you do read the newspaper, you are misinformed.

Mark Twain

Times have changed since Mark Twain was around. We have seen much progress made, and newspapers are not all that's available for public consumption. The "news" is everywhere in many forms. To read or not to read—to watch or not to watch—to listen or not to listen. Those are the questions. All of this seems to fall under the "Can't Win" category. I tend to stay in touch with *the* Informer. He *knows* what's going on, and I trust Him.

_____

_____

_____

_____

_____

_____

_____

_____

_____

_____

EXTRA! EXTRA! READ ALL ABOUT IT!

The Bible is still relevant for today. In fact, it is more up to date than tomorrow's newspaper.

I don't need to see tomorrow's up-to-date reports or watch the news to be able to determine the accuracy of this post. Can't argue with the truth, but so many people try to do it anyway. The Bible doesn't need revision or editing— it has stood the test of time.

_____

_____

_____

_____

_____

_____

_____

_____

_____

_____

_____

_____

_____

GOD DOES EVERYTHING BIGGER

Don't make what people did TO you bigger than what Jesus did FOR you. God wants to help us get to the place where—in every area of our lives and hearts—we come to realize what God has done for us is bigger than what others have done to us. Where what God has said about us is greater than what others have said about us or to us.

Christine Caine

This is the place to be. Everyone can go there if they're willing to choose the flight plan. It's all about attitude and altitude. You must go higher.

_____
_____
_____
_____
_____
_____
_____
_____
_____
_____

MASTERPIECE

I am the Potter, you are the clay.

Things go much better when you do things My way.

GOD

This is a great plan and has *always* worked out well for me. God continues to mold and shape me into what He has created me to be—His masterpiece.

_____

_____

_____

_____

_____

_____

_____

_____

_____

_____

_____

_____

_____

NOT ALONE

A single mother who trusts God is not raising her children alone.

Sometimes, in the middle of tough times, it's easy to forget about the decision we made to follow and trust God for everything. Raising kids well is an enormous undertaking, especially when trying to do it alone as a single parent. However, God has promised that He will never leave us or forsake us—even on the days when our kids are being oppositional, defiant, and disobedient. We are not alone.

_____

_____

_____

_____

_____

_____

_____

_____

_____

_____

_____

_____

_____

THE BUTTERFLY EFFECT

Every single thing you do matters.

You have been created as one-of-a-kind.

You have been created in order to make a difference.

You have within you the power to change the world!

Andy Andrews

There are so many people who don't believe this at all. It's easy to spot them because of the way they talk about themselves and because of their overall view of the world and their place in it. That's a sad commentary. If only they would be willing to accept that God has an assignment for each and every person on the planet, and everything they do matters on some level.

ARE YOU LISTENING?

Facing a difficult situation? It's one thing to have authority, it's another to hear from Heaven in how to use it in a particular situation. Many times, it's easy to get mechanical with your responses but remember, Jesus didn't always handle similar situations the same way each time.

This is where fellowship with and being led by the Holy Spirit comes into play. The reason Jesus always had success was because He only said what He heard the Father say and only did what He saw the Father do.

Because of our union with the Father and the Holy Spirit indwelling in us, we can hear and see in the exact same way and then use the authority Jesus gave us to get the results every single time.

Chad Gonzales

When the Holy Spirit is speaking, do you have your listening ears on? Selective hearing or not listening at all has gotten in the way of so many actions needing an obedient response but the follow-through was neglected.

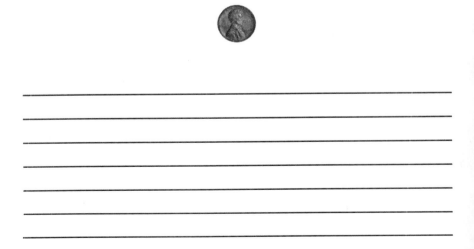

DAILY BREAD

The Bible is meant to be bread for daily use,

not cake for special occasions.

I would fail miserably if I ever tried to go on a keto or carb-free diet. *I love bread!* Jesus said, "I am the bread of life." (John 6:35)

I love Jesus! I can only imagine what my life would have been like without Him and His Word. My life has been directed by the Bible daily since Mother's Day 1971.

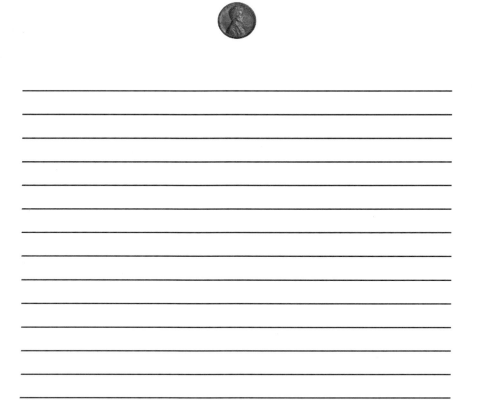

HEAVEN IS A REAL PLACE

Here are 10 truths about Heaven:

Heaven is a physical place with a specific location.

Rev. 12:22, 15:8, 19:14, 22:2

Heaven is a place of inexplicable joy – no more misunderstandings, isolating, hiding, or misinterpretations. Freedom from pain, sorrow, and sickness. Nothing to fear. No more rejection, failure, loss, or death. Perfect intimacy with God and others.

In Heaven, we'll be surrounded by God.

Heaven has an entry fee.

"If you confess with your mouth the Lord Jesus and believe in your heart that God raised Him from the dead, you will be saved." (Romans 10:9) This is our free pass to Heaven.

We'll have physical bodies.

2 Corinthians 5:1-4 says that, when our earthly body is destroyed, we'll receive an eternal body.

Believers enter immediately upon death. When we die, we either go to Heaven or to Hell for eternity. We face judgment (Hebrews 9:27). The criminal on the cross next to Jesus was told that he would be in paradise that day (Luke 23:43)

Heaven is eternal. This truth is reiterated throughout Scripture. Hell is also eternal (Matthew 25:46) Our eternal destination depends on whether or not we believe that God's Son is our Savior.

Heaven is incredibly diverse. God blessed all nations (Genesis 22:18). Rev. 7:9 says that "a great multitude...from every nation, tribe, people, and language" will worship together. All believers will be there.

We'll do more than sing. God's treasures of wisdom will be waiting for us to discover (Col. 2:3, Eph. 3:18-19). More than lifelong learners; learners for eternity.

We'll experience final victory over sin. In Heaven, we will finally experience full freedom from sin and will have the ability to live, think, and love as God desires.

Jennifer Slattery (abridged)

_____
_____
_____
_____
_____
_____
_____
_____
_____
_____
_____
_____

NOT A KNOW-IT-ALL

We don't know what we don't know. But what we don't know may present itself
as we loosen our grip on what we think we do know.

Robert Mann

Isn't it interesting that, as we are willing to open our mind to receive new ideas and truths, we begin to change our thinking by letting go of what we held dear and thought was right? Our beliefs and "truths" are challenged daily. Letting go of what we thought to be true in our own eyes by discovering we were wrong is a sign of maturity. The wisdom to make necessary adjustments to our thinking is the way to go.

And do not be conformed to this world, but be transformed
by the renewing of your mind, that you may prove what is
that good and acceptable and perfect will of God.
Romans 12:2 (NKJV)

_____

_____

_____

_____

_____

_____

_____

STORMY WEATHER

Some people create their own storms, then get upset when it rains!

Sometimes this starts out small—a little misstep here, a little ignored opportunity there—but before we know what's happening or how it gained such momentum so quickly, the storm is raging. It's times like these that remind us of how important the small details of life are and how much they matter. We are given the *response-ability* to handle whatever comes our way, especially if we are in a locked-in relationship with the One who is *The Way*. When we take our eyes off the Father and His plan for us, it's so easy to lose our way and veer off course. When that happens, we get afraid and desperate and understandably, upset.

But it's not too late to run for cover. Or to put it more succinctly, run to the Father who has us covered. Through our own negligence and carelessness, we create our own storms. But if we humbly *surrender* ourselves to the One who never leaves us or forsakes us, His love, grace, and guidance will restore us to a place of safety and great peace.

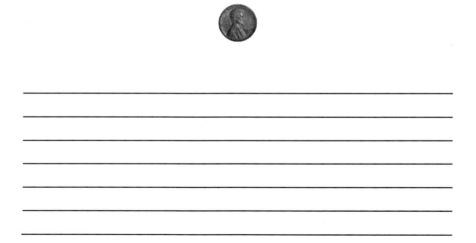

_____

_____

_____

_____

_____

_____

GRATEFUL HEART

If you can't have the best of everything,

make the best of everything you have.

G iving thanks with a grateful heart can be so hard when facing difficult challenges. I don't consistently do that very well. I especially have a very big ache in my heart when people I know and love are struggling. For some, there are actions they can choose to pursue to rectify what has gone "tilt" in their lives, but they are unwilling to commit to and follow through by doing the hard work to heal. On the other hand, a few of my very precious friends are facing mountains that are not of their own making. They need a miracle!

In both cases, I feel inadequate and powerless to bring about change and healing for them, but then I remember that it's not my job—it's a boundary issue. I can only be responsible for myself.

In the end, I need to focus on what's good with a grateful heart and lock arms with God and get after the other stuff as He leads me. Praying for the situations that others are facing is the most powerful tool that I have, so I use it a lot.

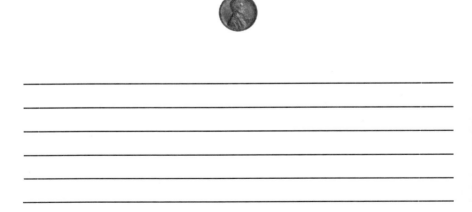

RECALCULATING

No matter how long you have traveled in the wrong direction,
you always have the choice to turn around.

Trulife

Recalculating! Recalculating! God's Positional System (GPS) announces that it's never too late to turn a life around and head it in the right direction. Consulting the Tour Guide who constructed the roads and planned out the best travel route would help.

WHAT DOES FAITH DO?

Faith doesn't always take you out of the problem;

Faith takes you through the problem.

Faith doesn't always take away the pain;

Faith gives you the ability to handle the pain.

Faith doesn't always take you out of the storm;

Faith calms you in the midst of the storm.

Hebrews 11 is known as the *Faith Chapter* with the first verse stating that faith is confidence in what we hope for and assurance about what we do not see. It goes on to mention the following faith-filled people: Abel, Enoch, Noah, Abraham, Sarah, Isaac, Jacob, Esau, Joseph, Moses, Rahab, Gideon, Samson, David, Samuel, the prophets, and more.

But without faith it is impossible to please Him, for he who comes to God must believe that He is and that He is a rewarder of those who diligently seek Him.
Hebrews 11:6 (NKJV)

The reward is taking us through problems, giving us the strength and ability to handle pain, and His presence calming us in the midst of life's many storms. Our responsibility is to diligently seek Him. Faith-filled believers are pleasing to God.

When faith is present, God moves on our behalf, but not always in the way we expect Him to move. He doesn't always remove problems, pain, or storms, but He does walk with us through everything. Faith is the anecdote for doubt and fear, and God is pleased when we exercise faith. Pleasing God is my goal so I will endeavor to operate in faith.

_____

_____

_____

_____

_____

_____

_____

_____

_____

_____

_____

_____

_____

_____

_____

_____

_____

_____

_____

_____

_____

_____

**For by grace you have been saved through faith, and that
not of yourselves; it is a gift of God, not of works, lest
anyone should boast.
Ephesians 2:8-9 (NKJV)**

PROCRASTINATION

It turns out procrastination is not typically a function of laziness, apathy or work ethic as it is often regarded to be. It's a neurotic self-defense behavior that develops to protect a person's sense of self-worth.

You see, procrastinators tend to be people who have, for whatever reason, developed to perceive an unusually strong association between their performance and their value as a person. This makes failure or criticism disproportionately painful, which leads naturally to hesitancy when it comes to the prospect of doing anything that reflects their ability... which is pretty much everything.

David Cain

Procrastination Is Not Laziness

Total inability to do just about anything. Wow! This explains a lot. David Cain identifies and labels procrastinators. Case closed. Nope, not so fast. This is a diagnosis, but is it permanent? It doesn't need to be. Is there a cure? Yes, there is. It will require a mirror and a lens adjustment. The way things are viewed are often skewed. People who procrastinate are labeled like Cain wrote, but why would anyone want to live with any of those negative labels?

Enter the Specialist (God). It's time to consult with Him, who is the only one who can evaluate and assign an individual's value. He determines that this diagnosis of procrastination can be temporary *if* the treatment plan is embraced and implemented. The Specialist explains that the diagnosis is a reason for inactivity, but it is not acceptable to settle into excuse mode. He tells the procrastinator that change is possible, and they are well able to change if they begin to see themselves with a different lens.

The fear of failure is real, but failure is inevitable in everyone's life. A major flip of the switch from "disproportionately painful" to "proportionally acceptable" is needed. Performance paralysis needs a regimen of emotional and spiritual therapy. Using the mirror and an eye chart will help the procrastinator begin to see more clearly. They will then begin to believe that they have what it takes to break the cycle of inactivity and start doing things. Trusting the Specialist and following His plan by doing the hard work results in *activity*.

_____
_____
_____
_____
_____
_____
_____
_____
_____
_____
_____
_____
_____
_____

I can do all things through Christ who strengthens me.
Philippians 4:13 (NKJV)

THE KNOWING

There will always be things we can't figure out, can't understand, and may never know the answer to, but our worst day with Jesus will always be better than our best day without Him.

Christine Caine

I've heard so many people say this for so many years. I used to think that was a stupid thing to say and utter nonsense. I'll bet almost everybody has had a really terrible day at least once so far—and there will probably be more on the horizon. That's life!

But here's the thing: When I was a young mother of two, I heard something that, through the years, proved to be absolutely true. When I accepted Jesus as my Lord, He promised to never leave me or forsake me, and He loved me like I'd never been loved before. There were times that I wandered off, but when I got in trouble and faced difficult situations, He was always there to pick me up. As a parent, I tried my best to be there for my kids when they were struggling—you know, kiss it and make it all better. Well, that's exactly what happens in my life. Because of my relationship with the Lord, just *knowing* that He is *always* with me no matter what makes everything better.

FROM PAIN TO PASSION

One of life's most important questions

"What will you do with your pain?"

You can numb yourself with denial and addictions, transfer your pain, inflicting it on others. You can hold it tightly, consumed inside by corrosive bitterness and explosive anger.

Or you can face it, going deep. Doing the work of transforming into a tender-hearted warrior, passionate about helping and healing others.

John Mack Green

If you truly wanted an answer to that question and asked my "bonus daughter," Molly, who went through unspeakable, horrendous pain and abuse in her life, she would say one word—*surrender*. She came to the end of herself and reached out to a Holy God for healing. Surrender is the key and the first step in the 12-Step Recovery Program. It is very difficult to totally surrender and yield to God when we think we can do whatever it takes to heal on our own. It's not easy to become vulnerable and dependent on someone other than ourselves, but God and others will help us to go deep and dig around the roots of our problems as we liberally sprinkle life-giving fertilizer for healing and growth where it's needed. It can be done.

When that happens, living with renewed hope and passion becomes so invigorating, and joy radiates out to others. Molly's passion for life and how God took her from a very dark, hopeless place into the light has been shared with so many people. And her journey, loaded with God's amazing grace and healing, has helped them have hope for their future.

Read more on Molly's story in the chapter, *She Believed She Could, So She Did.*

_____
_____
_____
_____
_____
_____
_____
_____
_____
_____
_____
_____
_____
_____
_____
_____
_____
_____
_____
_____
_____
_____

The Lord is my shepherd; I shall not want.
He makes me to lie down in green pastures; He leads me
beside the still waters. He restores my soul; He leads me in
the paths of righteousness for His name's sake.
Psalm 23:1-3 (ESV)

EYES FRONT AND CENTER

Satan's biggest fear is for you to become what God created you to be.
This is why he has tried everything to make you lose focus.

This almost sounds like a political statement, but don't look to the Left or to the Right. Keep your eyes steadfastly fixed on the One who *always* has something up His sleeve. If you're not watching, you'll miss it. He has a great plan for those who diligently seek Him and do what He says. This is not a time to allow distractions to get you sidetracked. The sky is not falling, and God is still on His throne. Keep your eye on the prize. *Focus!*

This wonderful song has been a calming reminder to me for many years. Here is the chorus:

Turn your eyes upon Jesus
Look full in His wonderful face
And the things of earth will grow strangely dim
In the light of His glory and grace

Helen H. Lemmel

_____

_____

_____

_____

_____

THE FLIPSIDE

We often hear:

"Life is short... better enjoy it."

How about:

"Eternity is long... better prepare for it."

We can really do both with gusto if we take care of the second part first. When our relocation is secured, we can go about enjoying our time here, knowing the best is yet to come.

GLUB, GLUB, GLUB

If you quit listening, dear child, and strike out on your own,

you'll soon be out of your depth.

Proverbs 19:27 (MSG)

This happens... sometimes prematurely. It's always wise to put on a lifejacket or have a lifeline within reach. When we think we have all the answers we need and turn a deaf ear to wise counsel and warnings, we realize, at some point, that we didn't know what we didn't know. Reach out for help before it's too late.

_____

_____

_____

_____

_____

_____

_____

_____

_____

_____

_____

_____

I'M WALKING & I'M TALKING

Tell, tell, tell what you know

Tell what you know to those who are near

Tell what you know to those who will hear

Tell it in words, words that are heard

Tell it in deeds, deeds that are seen

Tell to the lost and to those who are bound

Tell to the hopeless of what you have found

Do not withhold what's been given to you

The gift of Salvation and Words that are true

For you just may be the Light that one sees

The words that one hears, the words that one reads

Then hearing and seeing, some will respond

And know for themselves the love of your God

Guy Duininck

I'm walking and I'm talking... yes, indeed! As my time here is winding down, the cry of my heart is to bring as many with me as I can. My grands and great-grands are getting an earful these days. God has challenged me not to hold back at such a time as this. The world is in turmoil, and what the world needs now is love, sweet love—but not as the world gives. We need Jesus, the embodiment of love!

Here is one more piece of information that we all need to know. There is a wall of protection around Heaven, but there is also a *door*. We will be admitted if we hold the ticket to enter legally. Jesus paid the price for tickets for everyone and is willing to give us legal entry to a forever home called Heaven, but we must be willing to meet and accept the requirements. Be sure to get your *ticket to rise!*

_____

_____

_____

_____

_____

_____

_____

_____

_____

_____

_____

_____

_____

_____

_____

_____

_____

_____

_____

_____

_____

_____

Jesus answered and said to him (Nicodemus), "Most
assuredly, I say to you, unless one is born again, he cannot
see the kingdom of God."
John 3:3 (NKJV)

HANGING OUT WITH GOD

If you don't have a vision or dream for your life, it's simply because you haven't
been hanging out with God enough.

Chad Gonzales

For many years, I have gotten up in the morning and asked God what
we were going to be doing that day. I know I'm not in this thing called
life all alone, nor do I want to be. My trusted and safe Companion is God.
If I do anything, I want Him by my side doing it with me. That's what I
want, but truth be told, I haven't always included Him and taken Him on
some of my adventures. It doesn't take me very long to notice the
difference.

Things often lack purpose and my desired outcome when I do things on
my own. That's when I realize how badly I need God to remain an integral
part of my life 100% of the time. Visions and dreams are nonstop and so
indescribable when we do things together. When days like that come to
nightfall, I know beyond a shadow of a doubt that the day was well-spent.
Needless to say, hanging out with God is my favorite thing to do.

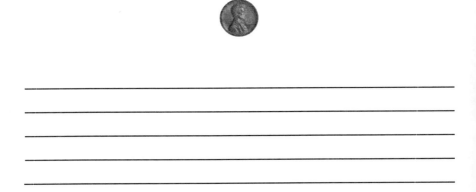

_____

_____

_____

_____

_____

ENJOY WHAT YOU DO

When I was 15, I spent a month working on an archeological dig. I was talking to one of the archeologists one day during our lunch break, and he asked those kinds of "getting to know you" questions you ask young people: Do you play sports? What's your favorite subject? And I told him, no, I don't play any sports. I do theater, I'm in choir, I play the violin and piano, I used to take art classes. And he went WOW. That's amazing! And I said, "Oh no, but I'm not any good at ANY of them.

And he said something then that I will never forget and which absolutely blew my mind because no one had ever said anything like it to me before: "I don't think being good at things is the point of doing them. I think you've got all these wonderful experiences with different skills, and that all teaches you things and makes you an interesting person, no matter how well you do them."

And that honestly changed my life. Because I went from a failure, someone who hadn't been talented enough at anything to excel, to someone who did things because I enjoyed them. I had been raised in such an achievement-oriented environment, so inundated with the myth of talent, that I thought it was only worth doing things if you could "Win" at them.

Kurt Vonnegut

What an interesting perspective. This is an encouragement to flap your wings and fly, even if you're not very good at it.

_____
_____
_____
_____
_____
_____
_____
_____
_____
_____
_____
_____
_____
_____
_____
_____
_____
_____
_____
_____
_____

And God is able to bless you abundantly, so that in all things at all times, having all that you need, you will abound in every good work.
II Corinthians 9:8 (NIV)

STOP WITH THE EXCUSES!

We as Christians need to stop using the "God is still working on me" line as an excuse to continue to justify doing the things we know are displeasing to God.

mybible.com

It *is* true that God is still working on us and, if we're honest, it appears that His work may never be done. But we need to ask a very important question. To what extent are *we* working *with* God to get the job done?

Making excuses for disobedience when we know better doesn't fly. How serious are we going to be about our commitment to Him when we *know* that He hasn't held back anything from us? When we know better, it's on us to do better. No more excuses. It's time for some full-on reciprocity.

_____

_____

_____

_____

_____

_____

_____

_____

_____

_____

THE BEST PARTNERSHIP

When God sees you doing your part, developing what He has given you, then He will do His part and open doors that no man can shut.

This is the "when-then" clause that calls for some personal responsibility and obedience. It's wise to remember who sets the criteria and calls the shots.

A WHOLE LOTTA SHAKING GOING ON

Sometimes our lives have to be completely shaken up, changed, and
rearranged to relocate us to the place we're meant to be.

Quotes 'n Thoughts

The book, *Changes That Heal* by Dr. Henry Cloud, is an invaluable
resource that helps shake things out and fall into place. The project
manager's name for this job is God, and even though we think we know
what we're doing and how to figure it all out on our own, His plan is
always superior to ours. If we are willing to do things His way, the
outcome will be perfect.

_____

_____

_____

_____

_____

_____

_____

_____

_____

_____

_____

PRICE CHECK

If you aren't being treated with love and respect,

check your price tag.

Maybe you've marked yourself down.

It's you who tells people what you're worth.

Get off the clearance rack and get behind the glass

where they keep the valuables.

I f you don't know how valuable you are, ask God. He is especially fond of you and thinks you have great value.

_____

_____

_____

_____

_____

_____

_____

_____

_____

_____

_____

_____

_____

YOU DECIDE

We are not given a good life or a bad life.

We are given a life.

It's up to us to make it good or bad.

Personal responsibility is the key. There are those who may not have had a great beginning for a variety of reasons, but as adults, it's up to every individual to maximize opportunities and become all they were created to be—no excuses. They might need a little help along the way though, and that is OK. God's Word makes it clear that this is part of His plan.

Take good counsel and accept correction – that's the way to live wisely and well.
Proverbs 19:20 (MSG)

Refuse good advice and watch your plans fail; take good counsel and watch them succeed.
Proverbs 15:22 (MSG)

Using wisdom is a component that is needed to live a good life. If we're serious about living a good life, we will take these passages to heart. On the road to developing this good life, we will need to connect with truly dependable people who are trustworthy and wise.

_____

_____

_____

_____

_____

_____

_____

_____

_____

_____

_____

_____

_____

_____

_____

_____

_____

_____

_____

_____

_____

_____

_____

**Trust in the Lord with all your heart, and lean not on your
own understanding. In all your ways acknowledge Him, and
He shall direct your paths.
Proverbs 3:5-6 (NKJV)**

THE TRUTH ABOUT TRUTH

No matter how long it takes or how desperately

a person battles or denies,

the truth always... always... makes itself known.

Andy Andrews

F reedom comes when the truth is revealed. In John 8:32, we are told that when we *know* the truth, it will set us free. We can stick our heads in the sand to avoid seeing it, we can argue against it, we can rationalize "living *our* truth," and we can even vehemently deny the truth, but *the* truth *is* the truth.

Truth lasts, lies are here today, gone tomorrow.
Proverbs 12:19 (MSG)

_____

_____

_____

_____

_____

_____

_____

_____

_____

_____

HAVE PATIENCE - DON'T BE IN SUCH A HURRY

Today we are obsessed with speed, but God is more interested in strength and stability than swiftness. We want the quick fix, the shortcut, the on-the-spot solution. We want a sermon, a seminar, or an experience that will instantly resolve all problems, remove all temptation, and release us from all growing pains. But real maturity is never the result of a single experience, no matter how powerful or moving.

Growth is gradual.

Rick Warren

Purpose Driven Life

With gradual growth, we will experience growing pains. Not all growth is easy. I can remember times of impatiently waiting for breakthroughs to happen and spouting off with, "Lord, give me patience, and I want it right now!" That was a prayer that many of my friends blurted out too, back in the day when we were young and immature Christians.

I have lost count on how many times God has asked me to do something, but I've kept Him waiting. And yet, He has been consistently patient with me. Over time, I have learned that God has an excellent plan for my life, and His Word says that He is never early and He's never late. His timing is *just right!* If patience really is a virtue, I need to get better at it. Since I am entering the "golden years" and I've slowed down considerably, the word "gradual" in the following scripture works very well for me.

Our lives gradually become brighter and more beautiful as God enters our lives and we become like Him.
2 Corinthians 3:18 (MSG)

_____

_____

_____

_____

_____

_____

_____

_____

_____

_____

_____

_____

_____

_____

_____

_____

_____

_____

_____

_____

_____

_____

But those who wait on the Lord shall renew their strength;
they shall mount up with wings like eagles, they shall run
and not be weary, they shall walk and not faint.
Isaiah 40:31 (NKJV)

SHAKE OFF APATHY

Nothing results from apathy.

Max Lucado

A pathy is defined as a lack of interest, enthusiasm, or concern. There is no motivation to do anything about anything. When we show indifference and a lack of caring about what's going on around us, nothing changes. The "value" of complacency in God's eyes is summed up well in Revelations:

> **So, because you are lukewarm, and neither hot nor cold, I**
> **will spit you out of My mouth.**
> **Revelations 3:16 (ESV)**

As my dad used to say, "It's time to pee or get off the pot!" *Do something!* Apathy is a waste of the precious time we have been given to accomplish much in this life. Shake off apathy and start living a life that matters. You only live once!

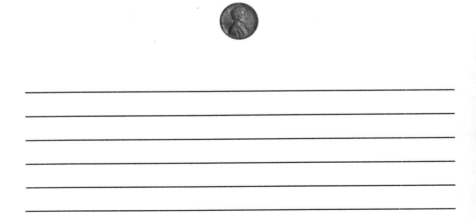

_____

_____

_____

_____

_____

_____

INTERCESSORY PRAYER IS POWERFUL

God often answers prayers that
we never even pray.

I am so thankful for intercessory prayers. My mom (and likely many others) prayed for me way back when—when I didn't have a clue. When my life lacked color and purpose, the faithful, fervent prayers of others opened the door to the place I needed to enter. God's mercy and amazing grace was extended to me, and *Godwinks* have been plentiful from that day on.

Don't get me wrong, there have been plenty of challenges and hard times too, but even when I didn't know I needed to pray or what to pray, God has been faithful. It is a true statement when I say that God has never left me or forsaken me.

Sometimes, when things have gone sideways in my life and I don't know what or how to pray, I'm like the little girl who prays by reciting the alphabet. She doesn't know what to say, but she trusts that God will arrange the letters and form a perfect prayer. He sees my heart and hears me even when I'm silent. God *knows* what I need. But here's the bottom line—*I need him!*

_____

_____

_____

THE B-I-B-L-E

A father was approached by his small son who told him proudly, "I know what the Bible means!"

His father smiled and replied, "What do you mean, you 'know what the Bible means'?"

The boy replied, "I do know!"

"Okay," said his father. "What does the Bible mean?"

"That's easy, Daddy..." the young boy replied excitedly.

"It stands for Basic Information Before Leaving Earth."

This lad nailed it! It's the best "How to" manual for successful living on this planet prior to relocation. The instructions are way more understandable and much easier to follow than some of the instructions the big box stores provide with their products. Quite frankly and literally, I would have been lost without my Bible—it has been the best road map for my life. And it will get me to where I really want to go!

TWO-WAY COMMUNICATION

Complaining about a silent God while your Bible is closed is like complaining about not getting texts when your phone is turned off.

The definition of communication is imparting or exchanging information. I much prefer a complete, two-way exchange. Without that, connecting feels incomplete to me. How often do we get ticked off when we know our text has been delivered and read, but no response is forthcoming?

God is always ready to answer us when we call, but it's up to us to keep our lines open. The Bible is one of the methods that God uses to speak to us and He even has answers to questions we have never even thought to ask. God speaks to us loud and clear through His Word as it is God-breathed. If we will simply take the time to read it, with a heart to hear, we will discover the truth—that there was never a time when God gave us the silent treatment.

_____

_____

_____

_____

_____

_____

_____

_____

LOVE REALLY DOESN'T HURT

Everyone says that love hurts, but that is not true.

Loneliness hurts.

Rejection hurts.

Losing someone hurts.

Envy hurts.

Everyone gets these things confused with love. But, in reality, love is the only thing in this world that covers up all pain and makes someone feel wonderful again.

Proper perspective can clear up common misconceptions. The problem might be that the word "love" is being misused and blamed for all the heartaches and abuses we see today. Perhaps it's time to go back to the origin of love—GOD IS LOVE. The way He loves and the way He has tried to show us how to love one another has been lost in our messed-up perceptions and misinterpretations of the real meaning of unconditional love. Real love covers a multitude of sins. (I Peter 4:8). Love doesn't hurt but lots of other things do. Stop lumping them all together and calling it love. It's not!

Real love *will* make it all better. Since God *is* Love, start there. He has open appointments and will meet with you at any time 24/7. If you really want to know what love is, ask God. Love is not the problem; love is the cure!

MY FAVORITE AUTHOR

The more you read the Bible, the more you'll love the Author.

I've been reading this book a lot since Mother's Day, some fifty years ago. It never fails to give fresh insight and it never gets old or boring. It's not like I wasn't familiar with it before then though. I grew up in a family that attended church twice on Sunday and once mid-week. We read the Bible at the dinner table, got to know all the hymns in church, and acknowledged there must be a God—Father, Son, and Holy Spirit. But here's the thing, I knew who God was, and it was reported through sermons and Sunday School lessons that He had done many great things, but I didn't *know him!* That's a big NO—an enormous difference. When I said yes and accepted what Jesus did on the cross for me, everything changed on that Mother's Day.

Numerous copies and translations of the Bible became my main reference source for how to live a full and joyful life with purpose. It wasn't just a good book, like so many others, with lots of helpful hints on how to live a good life. It was and has been my lifeline. There is no other book that comes close to the Bible. The more I read, the more I've been inspired to read more. People tell me about books that are so good that they can't put them down. I get it! I've had some of those too, but they pale by comparison to the Bible. It is the one book that helps me know God's heart better than any other. Every time I read familiar verses at different times in my life, they give me fresh insight and greater understanding. I feel closely connected to the Author. Nobody knows me like He does, and He reveals and shares Himself with me when I read the words that He has breathed into His Word. They are for my benefit, and His friendship, wisdom, guidance, and love is freely offered to me. I'll take it! *And I love Him too!* I sometimes like to say that I'm His favorite— but in reality, so are you!

_____

_____

_____

_____

_____

_____

_____

_____

_____

_____

_____

_____

_____

_____

_____

_____

_____

_____

_____

_____

_____

_____

_____

_____

_____

Your word is a lamp to my feet and a light to my path.
Psalm 119:105 (NKJV)

CONVERSATION WITH GOD

On Becoming

Me: Hey God.

God: Hello.

Me: I'm falling apart. Can You put me back together?

God: I'd rather not.

Me: Why?

God: Because you aren't a puzzle.

Me: What about all of the pieces of my life that are falling down onto the ground?

God: Let them stay there for awhile. They fell off for a reason. Take some time and decide if you need any of those pieces back.

Me: You don't understand. I'm breaking down!

God: No... you don't understand. You are breaking through. What you are feeling are just growing pains. You are shedding the things and the people in your life that are holding you back. You aren't falling apart. You are falling into place. Relax. Take some deep breaths and allow those things you don't need anymore to fall off of you. Quit holding onto the pieces that don't fit you anymore. Let them fall off. Let them go.

Me: Once I start doing that, what will be left of me?

God: Only the very best pieces of you.

Me: I'm scared of changing.

God: I keep telling you – YOU AREN'T CHANGING!! YOU ARE BECOMING!

Me: Becoming who?

God: Becoming who I created you to be! A person of light and love and clarity and hope and courage and joy and mercy and grace and compassion. I made you for more than the shallow pieces you have decided to adorn yourself with that you cling to with such greed and fear. Let those things fall off of you. I love you! Don't change!! Become! Become! Become who I made you to be. I'm going to keep telling you this until you remember it.

Me: There goes another piece.

God: Yep. Let it be.

Me: So... I'm not broken?

God: Of course not! But you are breaking like the dawn. It's a new day.

Become!

John Roedel

Aaah... so that is what's going on. This is all about perspective and looking at things in different ways. I've been using the word "change" for many years—as a psychologist, counselor, and leader of groups. For some groups, I've used the curriculum from a life-changing book with excellent insights and strategies for healing, *Changes That Heal,* by Dr. Henry Cloud.

There's nothing wrong with using the words "changing" or "becoming" really, it's just seeing what's going on from a different perspective. As a matter of fact, I frequently use the phrase "becoming all we were created to be." See, there it is—*becoming*. The idea of becoming is, well, quite becoming and appropriate when looking at it from this perspective.

God, the best Life Coach ever, uses both words frequently in His Word as He teaches us how to change, heal, and become all He has created us to be. Following His teachings and examples, I think I will continue to use both words and approaches using different perspectives too, as I encourage dear ones to make necessary *changes* to pursue *becoming* all they were created to be.

_____

_____

_____

_____

_____

_____

_____

_____

_____

_____

_____

_____

_____

_____

_____

_____

_____

_____

_____

_____

_____

_____

_____

God can do anything, you know --- far more than you could
ever imagine or guess or request in your wildest dreams! He
does it not by pushing us around but by working within us,
his Spirit deeply and gently within us.
Ephesians 3:20 (MSG)

MOTHER'S DAY 1971

I became a Christian on Mother's Day 1971. Growing up in the church made me religious; accepting Jesus as my personal Lord and Savior and Friend made that decision a lifetime *relationship*. Religion and relationship are NOT synonymous terms. The date is significant because it was my mom's prayers that broke down the barriers that gave me free access to Kingdom Living. I celebrate my born-again birthday every Mother's Day, the day my spirit was renewed! I'm still working on the soul part, but at least I have the best Tour Guide to lead me as I meander through this adventure called life.

My mom was the best at so many things and she loved me well no matter what, BUT—and this is a big "but," as you can see—the most wonderful thing that my prayer-warrior mother ever did for me was pray me into the Kingdom.

My mom relocated to Heaven in June 2005, and I think about her and miss her every day. Besides being my mom, she was a great friend of mine in so many ways. We were very blessed to be able to spend a lot of time together over the years, but especially in the final ten years or so of her life. Even though I miss her, I *know* she is having the time of her life with the Lord and with her family and friends who have also relocated. I look forward to hooking back up with her in the future, and I *know* that will happen due to the faithful and fervent prayers of my mom on my behalf. My mom was, and continues to be, the best! I love her a bushel and a peck!

This memory rolls around every year as Mother's Day approaches. This is super significant, because it is a very condensed testimony of how God used my mom to save my life—literally.

_____

_____

_____

_____

_____

_____

_____

_____

_____

_____

_____

_____

_____

_____

_____

_____

_____

_____

_____

_____

_____

**The effective, fervent prayer of a righteous man avails
much.**
James 5:16b (NKJV)

4

FINAL THOUGHTS

AFTERWORD

While working with Linda (Mom) on this project I wanted to capture her unique style of communication and humor while giving high respect to her years of wisdom. I trust you have come to know her more deeply and sensed her heart among these pages.

When researching the book cover ideas, I came across an interesting fact. In a most appropriate turn of fate, the year of my mother's birth, 1943, has a unique history regarding the minting of the penny. Who knew? This is so fitting because now that you know Linda, you understand how pleased she would be with the story that follows.

To support rationing certain metals during the wartime efforts, copper, which is used in the minting of pennies, was temporarily halted. During this special year, all pennies were to be stamped from steel and then coated with zinc. This created unique silvery one-cent pieces that appeared, at first glance, as a shiny dimes.

This fascinating turn of events reveals a dichotomy in how pennies of this era are now valued. Because some very common copper penny blanks were stuck in the stamping machines or in the corners of the coin blank totes since the year before, they were stamped with all the "special" steel pennies and entered the general coin population in that year. One might think, if you are now fortunate enough to find a silvery 1943 penny, you might have something of great worth, but you'd be wrong. Though a steel penny might now be worth a few dollars because of its novelty, due to the extreme rarity of a 1943 *copper* penny, if you were to find one like the one pictured on the cover of this book, it would be worth somewhere between 65 and 400 thousand dollars. Yes, you read that right.

I find it so fitting when considering the most mundane and common of items, the one-cent piece, that its worth can exceed the wildest imagination when its uniqueness is brought to light. The roughly 40 copper pennies that were minted during the year Mom was learning to walk have extreme value—not because they were simply forgotten blanks but because they were stamped into their full purpose, nonetheless.

We should remember this when we feel as though our lives do not seem to have value or that we are stuck in the forgotten places. The One who breathed into your first breath has never lost track of you, and He knows exactly how your life is to be minted into the immeasurable value which He already established from the foundation of time.

I am so grateful that you had a chance to meet my mother and hear her perspective seasoned by years of seeking to live for Christ. She would rightly say that even though we may have our flaws, our Savior speaks through us anyway and we should not discount or apologize for the importance of our words when they line up with the Word of God.

My prayer has always been that this compilation reaches much further than Mom ever dreamed. I'm confident it will. I find it refreshing that God uses our individuality and imperfections to successfully spread Kingdom principles through our circles of influence and then on to the far reaches of our world. Linda is fully aware of this truth and has sought to optimize her remaining time on this side of eternity in this pursuit—through writing as well as via her preferred method of interaction, the "one-on-one."

Finally, if you ever happen upon Linda during the course of your day, strike up a conversation. To her, this is what it's all about. Don't be surprised if she is quick to identify herself not by her vocation, education, or social standing, but simply by her proximity to the wind of the Spirit. I suggest we all strive to live likewise, as this is the only consistent place where *who we are* meets *who we can be*.

Forever in Christ—

Rusty James Rowgo
Host of *The Ride Podcast*

ABOUT ROWGO

Linda was born in Kalamazoo, Michigan a great many years ago. Still residing in the city of her youth, she has primarily been a Christian, mom, grandma (and oma), and friend. Vocationally, Linda has worn the hat of schoolteacher, limited license psychologist, high school counselor, and small group leader over the years. Her side gigs have included many interesting jobs—but that's a story for another day.

In 2006, Linda retired, but likes to refer to the time since as her *re-firement*. She continues to cherish times spent with friends and family, talking about things that matter, and building strong, priceless relationships. Teaching, counseling, encouraging, and loving others will continue to be the beat that goes on as long as Linda lives this side of eternity.

Her prayer has always been that after relocating to Heaven she will have left warm memories and lots of smiles behind. Beyond that, she hopes to see everyone again and likes to part with the words, *"To be continued..."*